DOVER · THRIFT · EDITIONS

Great Speeches

FRANKLIN DELANO ROOSEVELT

EDITED BY

JOHN GRAFTON

DOVER PUBLICATIONS, INC.
Mineola, New York

DOVER THRIFT EDITIONS

General Editor: Paul Negri
Editor of This Volume: John Grafton

Copyright

Copyright © 1999 by Dover Publications, Inc.
All rights reserved.

Bibliographical Note

This Dover edition, first published in 1999, is a new selection of the speeches of Franklin Delano Roosevelt made by John Grafton, who has also provided the Introduction and Historical Notes that precede each speech.

Library of Congress Cataloging-in-Publication Data

Roosevelt, Franklin D. (Franklin Delano), 1882–1945.
    Great speeches / Franklin Delano Roosevelt ; edited by John Grafton.
        p.   cm.
    ISBN-13: 978-0-486-40894-1
    ISBN-10: 0-486-40894-9
    1. United States—Politics and government—1933–1945. 2. Roosevelt, Franklin
D. (Franklin Delano), 1882–1945—Philosophy. 3. Speeches, addresses, etc.,
American.   I. Grafton, John.   II. Title.
E742.5.R65   1999
973.917'092—dc21
                                                                        99-31543
                                                                        CIP

Manufactured in the United States by Courier Corporation
40894904
www.doverpublications.com

Introduction

In the relatively short span of twenty-five years from his first national campaign in 1920 until his death in the first year of his fourth term as President in 1945, Franklin Delano Roosevelt gave hundreds and hundreds of speeches. He spoke as a private citizen, as a Democratic campaigner, as Governor of New York State, above all as President of the United States during the darkest years of the Depression, and as the acknowledged leader of the Free World in the global struggle against fascism. He was a masterful speaker, surely with few if any peers in that regard among American political figures before his time or since. He could be delightfully informal, imperiously statesmanlike, witheringly sarcastic, stern and serious when the occasion demanded, and even outright funny when it served his—usually political—purposes. Above all, he could communicate his ideas, even complicated and unpopular ideas, directly and to the point, convincingly and thoroughly. Many who heard him, in person or on the radio (which really was his medium), record that he succeeded in doing what many speakers try and which few accomplish: Although his audiences may have often included more than thirty million people just in America, and millions more around the world, listeners often felt he was speaking to them alone.

In the brief collection presented here, it has only been possible to record some of the many high spots from Roosevelt's life as a speaker including inaugural addresses, some historical milestones such as the War Message to Congress the day after the attack on Pearl Harbor, and several of his unique "Fireside Chats." This collection mirrors the course of FDR's life in office. After a few early speeches from the years before he was first elected president in 1932, there follow several where he set forth the philosophy and programs of the New Deal. Toward the end of the 1930s, the scene changes to speeches on the international

political scene, and finally to the conduct of World War II itself. No
collection like this would be complete, however, without something
from Roosevelt the pure politician, and so the famous "Fala" speech
at the Teamsters Union dinner in 1944 was selected to serve as an
example which could have been multiplied many times over. Only one
of his hundreds of recorded press conferences could be included here,
the memorable elucidation of the concept of "Lend-Lease." Many en-
tertaining and historically significant volumes equal in size to this one
could be compiled from his White House press conferences alone.

Roosevelt worked very hard on his speeches, and those who worked
for him always worked hard on them as well through draft after draft,
revision after revision, often right up to the last possible moment.
Whatever their individual purposes, they were thoughtful, finished
statements, always polished and sharpened to a fine point of exposition.
Taken together, they provide an indispensable window onto the history
of FDR's time.

—John Grafton

Contents

Acceptance Speech For Vice-Presidential Nomination
Hyde Park, August 9, 1920

FDR began his career in public life serving in the New York State Senate from 1911 to 1913. He gained prominence as Woodrow Wilson's Assistant Secretary of the Navy from 1913 to 1920, spending the whole of World War I in that capacity. He was a sufficiently visible Democrat to receive the party's vice presidential nomination in 1920 on the ticket led by James M. Cox of Ohio, although he was only thirty-eight years old at the time. Following the time-honored practice of candidates not appearing at their party's nominating conventions, FDR accepted the Democratic nomination for the vice-presidency with this speech delivered at Hyde Park on August 9, 1920.

Despite the conservative trend the country was taking, Roosevelt enthusiastically identified himself with the Wilsonian-Progressive wing of the Democratic party and made United States entry into the League of Nations his central issue. The electorate rejected the League and the Democrats, sending Warren Harding to the White House and FDR back to New York and the private practice of law. For FDR, the 1920 campaign was a setback in his political career which no doubt seemed permanent to many when he contracted infantile paralysis the following year while vacationing at the Roosevelt summer home on Campobello Island off the coast of New Brunswick.

I accept the nomination for the office of Vice-President with humbleness, and with a deep wish to give to our beloved country the best that is in me. — No one could receive a higher privilege or opportunity than to be thus associated with men and ideals which I am confident will soon receive the support of the majority of our citizens.

In fact, I could not conscientiously accept it if I had not come to know by the closest intimacy that he who is our selection for the Presidency, and who is my chief and yours, is a man possessed of ideals which are also mine. He will give to America that kind of leadership which will make us respect him and bring further greatness to our land. In him I recognize one who can lead this nation forward in an unhalting march of progress. Such a man is James M. Cox.

Two great problems will confront the next administration; our relations with the world and the pressing need of organized progress at home. The latter includes a systematized and intensified development of our resources and a progressive betterment of our citizenship. These matters will require the guiding hand of a President who can see his country above his party, and who, having a clear vision of things as they are, has also the independence, courage and skill to guide us along the road to things as they should be without swerving one footstep at the dictation of narrow partisans who whisper "party" or of selfish interests that murmur "profits."

In our world problems, we must either shut our eyes, sell our newly built merchant marine to more far-seeing foreign powers, crush utterly by embargo and harassing legislation our foreign trade, close our ports, build an impregnable wall of costly armaments and live, as the Orient used to live, a hermit nation, dreaming of the past; or, we must open our eyes and see that modern civilization has become so complex and the lives of civilized men so interwoven with the lives of other men in other countries as to make it impossible to be in this world and not of it. We must see that it is impossible to avoid, except by monastic seclusion, those honorable and intimate foreign relations which the fearful-hearted shudderingly miscall by that Devil's catch word "international complications."

As for our home problem, we have been awakened by this war into a startled realization of the archaic shortcomings of our governmental machinery and of the need for the kind of reorganization which only a clear thinking business man, experienced in the technicalities of governmental procedure, can carry out. Such a man we have. One who has so successfully reformed the business management of his own great State is obviously capable of doing greater things. This is not [the] time to experiment with men who believe that their party can do no wrong and that what is good for the selfish interests of a political party is of necessity good for the nation as well. I as a citizen believe that this year we should choose as President a proven executive. — We need to do things; not talk about them.

Much has been said of late about good Americanism. It is right that it should have been said, and it is right that every chance should be seized to repeat the basic truths underlying our prosperity and our national existence itself. — But it would be an unusual and much to be wished for thing, if, in the coming presentation of the issues a new note of fairness and generosity could be struck. Littleness, meanness, false-hood, extreme partisanship—these are not in accord with the American spirit. I like to think that in this respect also we are moving forward.

Let us be definite. We have passed through a great war,—an armed conflict which called forth every effort on the part of the whole popu-lation.—The war was won by Republicans as well as by Democrats. Men of all parties served in our armed forces.—Men and women of all parties served the government at home. They strived honestly as Americans, not as mere partisans. Republicans and Democrats alike worked in administrative positions, raised Liberty loans, administered food control, toiled in munition plants, built ships.—The war was brought to a successful conclusion by a glorious common effort—one which in the years to come will be a national pride. I feel very certain that our children will come to regard our participation as memorable for the broad honor and honesty which marked it, for the absence of unfortunate scandal, and for the splendid unity of action which ex-tended to every portion of the nation. It would, therefore, not only serve little purpose,—but would conform ill to our high standards if any per-son should in the heat of political rivalry seek to manufacture political advantage out of a nationally conducted struggle. We have seen things on too large a scale to listen in this day to trifles, or to believe in the ad-equacy of trifling men.

It is that same vision of the bigger outlook of national and individual life which will, I am sure, lead us to demand that the men who repre-sent us in the affairs of our government shall be more than politicans or the errand boys of politicans—that they shall subordinate always the individual ambition and the party advantage to the national good. In the long run the true statesman and the honestly forward looking party will prevail.

Even as the Nation entered the war for an ideal, so it has emerged from the war with the determination that the ideal shall not die. It is idle to pretend that the war declaration of April 6th, 1917, was a mere act of self-defense,—or that the object of our participation was solely to defeat the military power of the Central Nations of Europe. We knew then as a Nation, even as we know today, that success on land and sea could be but half a victory. The other half is not won yet. To the cry of the French at Verdun; "They shall not pass"; the cheer of our own men in the Argonne; "We shall go through"—we must add this; "It shall not occur again." This is the positive declaration of our own wills; that the world shall be saved from a repetition of this crime.

To this end the democratic party offers a treaty of peace, which, to make it a real treaty for a real peace MUST include a League of Nations;

because this peace treaty, if our best and bravest are not to have died in vain, must be no thinly disguised armistice devised by cynical statesmen to mask their preparations for a renewal of greed-inspired conquests later on. "Peace" must mean peace that will last. A practical, workable, permanent, enforcible kind of a peace that will hold as tightly as the business contracts of the individual. We must indeed be, above all things, businesslike and practical in this peace treaty making business of ours. The League of Nations is a practical solution of a practical situation. It is no more perfect than our original Constitution, which has been amended 18 times and will soon, we hope, be amended the 19th, was perfect. It is not anti-national, it is anti-war. No super-nation, binding us to the decisions of its tribunals, is suggested, but the method and machinery by which the opinion of civilization may become effective against those who seek war is at last within the reach of humanity. Through it we may with nearly every other duly constituted government in the whole world throw our moral force and our potential power into the scale of peace. That such an object should be contrary to American policy is unthinkable; but if there be any citizen who has HONEST—and I emphasize the word honest—fears that it may be perverted from its plain intent so as to conflict with our established form of government, it will be simple to declare to him and to the other nations that the Constitution of the United States is in every way supreme. There must be no equivocation, no vagueness, no double dealing with the people on this issue. The League will not die. An idea does not die which meets the call of the hearts of our mothers.

So, too, with peace. War may be "declared"; peace cannot. It must be established by mutual consent, by a meeting of the minds of the parties in interest. From the practical point of view alone a peace by resolution of Congress is unworkable. From the point of view of the millions of splendid Americans who served in that whirlwind of war, and of those other millions at home who saw, in our part of the conflict, the splendid hope of days of peace for future generations, a peace by resolution of Congress is an insult and a denial of our national purpose.

Today we are offered a seat at the table of the family of nations to the end that smaller peoples may be truly safe to work out their own destiny, to the end that the sword shall not follow on the heels of the merchant, to the end that the burden of increasing armies and navies shall be lifted from the shoulders of a world already staggering under the weight of taxation. We shall take that place. I say so because I have faith—faith that this nation has no selfish destiny, faith that our people are looking into the years beyond for better things, and that they are not afraid to do their part.

The fundamental outlook on the associations between this Republic and the other Nations can never be very different in character from the principles which one applies to our own purely internal affairs. A man who opposes concrete reforms and improvements in international relations is of necessity a reactionary, or at least a conservative in viewing his home problems. . . .

Some people have been saying of late: "We are tired of progress, we want to go back to where we were before; to go about our own business; to restore 'normal' conditions of 'normalcy.'" They are wrong. This is not the wish of America! We can never go back. The "good old days" are gone past forever; we have no regrets. For our eyes are trained ahead—forward to better new days. In this faith I am strengthened by the firm belief that women of this nation, now about to receive the National franchise, will throw their weight into the scale of progress and will be unbound by partisan prejudices and a too narrow outlook on national problems. We cannot anchor our ship of state in this world tempest, nor can we return to the placid harbor of long years ago. We must go forward or founder.

America's opportunity is at hand. We can lead the world by a great example, we can prove this nation a living, growing thing, with policies that are adequate to new conditions. In a thousand ways this is our hour of test. The Democratic program offers a larger life for our country, a richer destiny for our people. It is a plan of hope. In this, chiefly let it be our aim to build up, not to tear down. Our opposition is to the things which once existed, in order that they may never return. We oppose money in politics, we oppose the private control of national finances, we oppose the treating of human beings as commodities, we oppose the saloon-bossed city, we oppose starvation wages, we oppose rule by groups or cliques. In the same way we oppose a mere period of coma in our national life. . . .

It is the faith which is in me that makes me very certain that America will choose the path of progress and set aside the doctrines of despair, the whispering of cowardice, the narrow road to yesterday. May the Guiding Spirit of our land keep our feet on the broad road that leads to a better tomorrow and give to us strength to carry on.

Campaign Speech
Buffalo, October 20, 1928

FDR's political comeback from polio and the 1920 defeat began at the Democratic convention of 1924 when he nominated his close friend, New York Governor Alfred E. Smith for the presidency, christening him "The Happy Warrior of the political battlefield." Smith failed to win the nomination, which after 102 bitterly contested ballots went to John W. Davis; but the fact that even with his disability FDR could make such a huge effort so successfully helped to put him back in the political limelight. In 1928, FDR nominated Smith again, and this time the "Happy Warrior" won the party's nomination. Smith and many other Democrats convinced FDR to run for governor of New York in the hope that FDR's popularity would help the party carry the state, crucial to any chance the Democrats had of national victory. FDR won the governorship by a narrow 25,000 vote margin, but Smith failed to carry New York State and lost the presidential election to Herbert Hoover.

In this campaign speech at Buffalo on October 20, 1928, Roosevelt engaged in the fierce political infighting which he always relished, bluntly accusing his opponents of lying to the public on the subject of support for labor. The speech is most interesting, however, for the plea for religious toleration with which it ends. However, the idea of electing a "wet" (anti-Prohibition) Catholic to the presidency in 1928 was probably a lost cause from day one; and despite the efforts of Roosevelt and others in this area, there is little doubt that Smith's religion cost him heavily in the election.

In a pigeon hole in the desk of the Republican leaders of New York State is a large envelope, soiled, worn and bearing a date that goes back twenty-five years. Printed in large letters on this envelope are the words "Promises to Labor." Inside the envelope are a series of sheets dated two years apart and representing the best thought of the best minds of the

Republican leaders over the succession of years. Each sheet of promises is practically a duplicate of every other sheet. Nowhere in that envelope is there a single page bearing the title "Promises Kept."

I ought to know something about it personally, because I had the good fortune to be a member of the State Senate in that famous year of 1911 when the Democratic Party, coming into control of the State government for the first time in a generation, started on its way a program, not of promises but of accomplishments.

The set-up in 1911 was exactly the same as it is in 1928. The Democratic administration and the Democratic leaders in the legislature began at that time a series of practical measures in the interest of the men and women of this State who work with their hands. That session of the legislature was the "Godfather" of the Workmen's Compensation Law, of the first law limiting the hours of women in industry, of the Factory Investigation Committee, and of a series of important measures strengthening the provisions of the existing labor law and building up the effective strength of the Labor Department.

It is worthwhile to go back as far as 1911 because we get at that time a definite picture of the attitude of the leaders of the two parties—an attitude which has continued down to the present day.

I remember well that the position of the Democratic Party was at that time severely criticized by the reactionary element in this State as being socialistic and radical, and if the term Bolshevist had been then in existence it would undoubtedly have been applied to Assemblyman Alfred E. Smith, Senator Robert Wagner and many others, including myself, because of our ardent support for the whole program.

Arrayed against us was the silent, powerful pressure of the old school of thought, which held to the theory that when an employer hired working men or working women, that employer became the master of the fate of his employees; that when a worker entered the factory doors it was nobody's business as to how he worked, how long he was worked or how much he was paid.

It is most difficult seventeen years later for this generation to understand the attitude of the old conservative element towards employment back in 1911, but it is a fact that this attitude was subscribed to sometimes silently sometimes openly but always definitely by the Republican leaders of this State at that time.

During the years 1911 to 1915, the splendid record of definite accomplishment made by the Democratic Party in this State was fought and blocked and criticized at every turn by the Republican legislative leaders.

The best example of the difference in attitude between the two parties is the fact that during the four years of Governor Whitman, constructive labor legislation in the State of New York came to an end. The progress was not resumed until Governor Smith went back to Albany as the Chief Executive in 1919.

In this year of 1928 it would have been possible to forecast last May with absolute exactitude what the Republican leaders and the Republican candidate would say during this autumn's campaign. First of all, they would trot out the old envelope, dust it off and copy into their platform the same old words which had been used every two years for a generation back. Let me read you the labor plank of the Republican Party:

"The Republican Party in this State has done more for labor than any other party. The Labor Law and the Workmen's Compensation Law, conceded by labor to be the best in all the states, almost every line has been written in these laws by or with the approval of our party."

How dare they say that?

How do grown up and ostensibly sane political leaders perjure themselves that way? For a statement of that kind is so openly and flagrantly dishonorable that it comes pretty close to the border line of perjury. These same leaders know perfectly well that the Republican Party has consistently fought against almost every progressive measure in the interests of labor that the State of New York has added to its statute books during the past seventeen years. . . .

Let us take the practical example of the principle of limiting the hours of work of women and children in industry. Back in that session of 1911 the Democratic leaders brought forward what was then regarded as the "radical" "socialistic" proposal limiting the hours to fifty-four a week. The record shows that the opposition came from the Republican leaders, but after a long fight the proposal became law.

When Alfred E. Smith went back to Albany as Governor in 1919 progressive thought had advanced to the point of demanding a further limitation for the women and children to a maximum of forty-eight hours a week. Through six years the demand for action increased and in 1924 the Republican State platform for the first time came out definitely in favor of a forty-eight hour week. It is almost needless to say that the Democratic platform again and yet again supported that demand.

It seemed, therefore, that the workers were definitely assured by both parties of the passage of the proposed law. Definite assurance was given to the voters of this State by Theodore Roosevelt, Jr., and the Republican leaders that they would carry out that pledge. What happened? The Republican legislature of 1925 failed utterly to carry out this plan, in spite of the demand for it by every Democratic member and by the Governor of the State. As a deliberate subterfuge, the Republican legislature passed the Joiner Bill, which was unanimously opposed by Labor and was characterized by the Governor as a "fraud upon the people of the State." Another promise gone bad! . . .

I want to add only one additional fact about myself. For seven and one-half years, as the Assistant-Secretary of the Navy, I had full charge of all matters relating to the subject of labor in the navy yards of the United States. The Navy was the direct employer of more than twenty thousand civilians during the peace period, and of more than one hundred thousand civilians during the war period. Up to 1913 the relations between the Government and its civilian employees had been precarious and filled with constant disputes. I shall always be very proud of the fact that from 1913 to the time I left the Navy Department in 1920, the United States Navy never had a single strike or a single serious dispute with the civilians in the Navy Yards, and the whole system of Navy Yard civilian employment was brought up to a far higher standard than ever before. . . .

If I am elected Govenor, it will of course be difficult to carry out the present splendid program of the Democratic Party, unless at the same time our party is in control of the Senate and of the Assembly. At least you can feel confident that I would use every effort to obtain legislation from a hostile legislature. . . .

And now one final word—the last time I expect to speak it in this campaign. Some misguided people in every section of the land have been violating by written or spoken word the Sixth Amendment to the Constitution of the United States, that great charter which forbids any religious test for the holding of public office. I hope and believe that as election day approaches this question will be left out of the decision of the electorate. Just as I have begged up and down the land that no vote be given to Hoover because his opponent is a member of another church of God, so I plead that no vote be given to me because my opponent is a member of a different church of God.

Message to the New York State Legislature
Albany, August 28, 1931

In his first term as governor of New York State (at that time, it was a two-year term), FDR saw his popularity increase beyond even his usually buoyant expectations, and he easily won reelection in 1930, this time by a huge 700,000-vote margin. As the country slid into the depths of the Depression, Roosevelt had a chance to try out in New York many of the ideas and programs that would later comprise major aspects of the New Deal. In his August 28, 1931 message to the New York State legislature, FDR delineated the need for greatly expanded funds to assist the destitute.

What is the State? It is the duly constituted representative of an organized society of human beings, created by them for their mutual protection and well-being. "The State" or "The Government" is but the machinery through which such mutual aid and protection are achieved. The cave man fought for existence unaided or even opposed by his fellow man, but today the humblest citizen of our State stands protected by all the power and strength of his Government. Our Government is not the master but the creature of the people. The duty of the State toward the citizens is the duty of the servant to its master. The people have created it; the people, by common consent, permit its continual existence.

One of these duties of the State is that of caring for those of its citizens who find themselves the victims of such adverse circumstance as makes them unable to obtain even the necessities for mere existence without the aid of others. That responsibility is recognized by every civilized Nation.

For example, from the earliest days of our own country the consciousness of the proper relationship between the State and the citizen resulted in the establishment of those often crude and unscientific but wholly necessary institutions known as the county poor houses.

In many messages to your Honorable Bodies I have pointed out that this earlier exemplification of the State's responsibility has been sustained and enlarged from year to year as we have grown to a better understanding of government functions. I have mentioned specifically the general agreement of today, that upon the State falls the duty of protecting and sustaining those of its citizens who, through no fault of their own, find themselves in their old age unable to maintain life.

But the same rule applies to other conditions. In broad terms I assert that modern society, acting through its Government, owes the definite obligation to prevent the starvation or the dire want of any of its fellow men and women who try to maintain themselves but cannot.

While it is true that we have hitherto principally considered those who through accident or old age were permanently incapacitated, the same responsibility of the State undoubtedly applies when widespread economic conditions render large numbers of men and women incapable of supporting either themselves or their families because of circumstances beyond their control which make it impossible for them to find remunerative labor. To these unfortunate citizens aid must be extended by Government, not as a matter of charity, but as a matter of social duty.

It is true beyond question that aid must be and will be given in large measure through the agencies of private contributions; and in normal times these contributions should be regarded as sufficient to meet normal conditions. However, even here the appeal is not alone on the basis of charity, but is laid on the foundation of the civic duty of all good citizens.

I would not be appearing before you today if these were normal times. When, however, a condition arises which calls for measures of relief over and beyond the ability of private and local assistance to meet—even with the usual aid added by the State—it is time for the State itself to do its additional share.

As my constitutional duty to communicate to your Honorable Bodies the condition of the State, I report to you what is a matter of common knowledge—that the economic depression of the last two years has created social conditions resulting in great physical suffering on the part of many hundreds of thousands of men, women and children. Unless conditions immediately and greatly change, this will, we fear, be aggravated by cold and hunger during the coming winter.

The many reports which I have received from municipal officials, from the Governor's Commission on the Stabilization of Employment, from the State Department of Social Welfare, and from many private organizations for relief and charity, agree that the number of our citizens who, this coming winter, will be in need will, so far as it is possible to estimate, be nearly, if not quite, twice as many as during the winter of 1930–1931.

There are many causes. Many individuals and families, because of prolonged unemployment, have exhausted their savings and their credit. Many who were at work last winter and were enabled to take care of their relatives and friends are now themselves out of work. In the same way, many employers who, up to recently, with fine public spirit have continued to use their resources to prevent the laying-off of workers, are finding that they can no longer do so. . . .

There is no escaping the simple conclusion that very large additional funds must be looked for this winter to supplement the lines of assistance given last year. . . .

Acceptance Speech
Chicago, July 2, 1932

Although FDR was certainly the nation's most prominent Democrat in the Depression summer of 1932, and his nomination for the presidency was in many ways a foregone conclusion, drama was provided at the Chicago convention by the rule which required victory by a two-thirds majority. Although there was no other candidate with anything like Roosevelt's hold on the imagination of the Democratic party, it took several ballots and many hours of skillful politicking by Roosevelt's able operatives to put him over the top. The decisive push came in part from an unlikely source, conservative press baron William Randolph Hearst, who controlled the California delegation, and who—along with House Speaker John Nance Garner—held sway with the delegates from Texas as well. While Roosevelt monitored events from Albany, his team in Chicago deftly persuaded Hearst and his allies that if FDR's support should wane as ballots came and went without a winner, they might be faced with the prospect of a compromise candidate they liked even less than FDR—for example, Newton D. Baker, a progressive, internationalist alumnus of the Wilson administrations. Hearst and Garner gave in and passed the word to the convention floor to end the suspense. Shortly thereafter, Roosevelt's 942 votes on the fourth ballot gave him the nomination. Garner was rewarded with the nomination for vice-president, and although reluctant to abandon the powerful speakership, accepted it for the good of the party.

It was not the practice in American politics up to that time for even successful candidates to appear at their party's nominating conventions. They would wait at home and at some point, sometimes weeks later, a suitable delegation would arrive from the national party and officially inform them of what everybody already knew—that they were their party's choice. FDR wanted to break with tradition with a bold statement, and he did this by flying to Chicago immediately after his victory to personally address the convention and accept the nomination. With unexpectedly strong headwinds and the need for several refueling stops, the flight from Albany to Chicago itself became a nine-hour epic which only served to heighten the drama. Arriving in Chicago, FDR reviewed drafts of acceptance speeches, taking his opening from a version prepared by his long-time political right hand, Louis Howe; but most of it derived from a draft he had worked on himself with another seasoned advisor, Samuel I. Rosenman. Drawing on a theme and an expression they had used before but which had not yet become their watchword—"I pledge you, I pledge myself to a new deal for the American people"—they gave the Democratic campaign of 1932 and their future administration its slogan and its definition. The following day the term "New Deal" was enshrined by the press when it was worked into a political cartoon by the widely syndicated artist, Rollin Kirby.

Chairman Walsh, my friends of the Democratic National Convention of 1932:

I appreciate your willingness after these six arduous days to remain here, for I know well the sleepless hours which you and I have had. I regret that I am late, but I have no control over the winds of Heaven and could only be thankful for my Navy training.

The appearance before a National Convention of its nominee for President, to be formally notified of his selection, is unprecedented and unusual, but these are unprecedented and unusual times. I have started out on the tasks that lie ahead by breaking the absurd traditions that the candidate should remain in professed ignorance of what has happened for weeks until he is formally notified of that event many weeks later.

My friends, may this be the symbol of my intention to be honest and to avoid all hypocrisy or sham, to avoid all silly shutting of the eyes to the truth in this campaign. You have nominated me and I know it, and I am here to thank you for the honor.

Let it also be symbolic that in so doing I broke traditions. Let it be from now on the task of our Party to break foolish traditions. We will break foolish traditions and leave it to the Republican leadership, far more skilled in that art, to break promises.

Let us now and here highly resolve to resume the country's interrupted march along the path of real progress, of real justice, or real equality for all of our citizens, great and small. Our indomitable leader in that interrupted march is no longer with us, but there still survives today his spirit. Many of his captains, thank God, are still with us, to give us wise counsel. Let us feel that in everything we do there still lives with us, if not the body, the great indomitable, unquenchable, progressive soul of our Commander-in-Chief, Woodrow Wilson. . . .

Wild radicalism has made few converts and the greatest tribute that

I can pay to my countrymen is that in these days of crushing want there persists an orderly and hopeful spirit on the part of the millions of our people who have suffered so much. To fail to offer them a new chance is not only to betray their hopes but to misunderstand their patience.

To meet by reaction that danger of radicalism is to invite disaster. Reaction is no barrier to the radical. It is a challenge, a provocation. The way to meet that danger is to offer a workable program of reconstruction, and the Party to offer it is the party with clean hands.

This, and this only is a proper protection against blind reaction on the one hand and an improvised hit-or-miss, irresponsible opportunism on the other.

There are two ways of viewing the government's duty in matters affecting economic and social life. The first sees to it that a favored few are helped and hopes that some of their prosperity will leak through, sift through, to labor, to the farmer, to the small businessman. That theory belongs to the party of Toryism, and I had hoped that most of the Tories left this country in 1776.

But it is not and never will be the theory of the Democratic Party. This is no time for fear, for reaction or for timidity. And here and now I invite those nominal Republicans who find that their conscience cannot be squared with the groping and the failure of their party leaders to join hands with us; here and now, in equal measure, I warn those nominal Democrats who squint at the future with their faces turned toward the past, and who feel no responsibility to the demands of the new time, that they are out of step with their party.

Yes, the people of this country want a genuine choice this year, not a choice between two names for the same reactionary doctrine. Ours must be a Party of Liberal thought, of planned action, of enlightened international outlook, and of the greatest good to the greatest number of our citizens. . . .

Statesmanship and vision, my friends, require relief to all at the same time.

Just one word or two on taxes, the taxes that all of us pay toward the cost of government of all kinds.

Well, I know something of taxes. For three long years I have been going up and down this country preaching that government—federal and state and local—costs too much. I shall not stop that preaching. As an immediate program of action we must abolish useless offices. We must eliminate actual functions of government—functions, in fact, that are not definitely essential to the continuance of government. We must merge, we must consolidate subdivisions of government, and, like the private citizen, give up luxuries which we can no longer afford.

By our example at Washington itself, we shall have the opportunity of pointing the way of economy to local government, for let us remember well that out of every tax dollar in the average state in this nation, 40 cents enters the treasury in Washington, D.C., 10 or 12 cents only go to the state capitals, and 48 cents out of every dollar are consumed by the costs of local government in counties and cities and towns.

I propose to you, my friends, and through you, that government of all kinds, big and little, be made solvent and that the example be set by the President of the United States and his Cabinet.

And talking about setting a definite example, I congratulate this convention for having had the courage, fearlessly, to write into its declaration of principles what an overwhelming majority here assembled really thinks about the 18th Amendment. This convention wants repeal. Your candidate wants repeal. And I am confident that the United States of America wants repeal.

Two years ago the platform on which I ran for Governor the second time contained substantially the same provision. The overwhelming sentiment of the people of my State, as shown by the vote of that year, extends, I know, to the people of many of the other States. I say to you now that from this date on the 18th Amendment is doomed. When that happens, we as Democrats must and will, rightly and morally, enable the States to protect themselves against the importation of intoxicating liquor where such importation may violate their State laws. We must rightly and morally prevent the return of the saloon. . . .

What do the people of America want more than anything else? In my mind, two things: Work; work, with all the moral and spiritual values that go with work. And with work, a reasonable measure of security—security for themselves and for their wives and children. Work and security—these are more than words. They are more than facts. They are the spiritual values, the true goal toward which our efforts of reconstruction should lead. These are the values that this program is intended to gain; these are the values we have failed to achieve by the leadership we now have.

Our Republican leaders tell us economic laws—sacred, inviolable, unchangeable—that these laws cause panics which no one could prevent. But while they prate of economic laws, men and women are starving. We must lay hold of the fact that economic laws are not made by nature. They are made by human beings.

Yes, when—not if—when we get the chance, the Federal Government will assume bold leadership in distress relief. For years Washington has alternated between putting its head in the sand and saying there is no large number of destitute people in our midst who need food and clothing, and then saying the States should take care of them, if there are. Instead of planning two and a half years ago to do what they are now trying to do, they kept putting it off from day to day and week to week, and month to month, until the conscience of America demanded action.

I say that while primary responsibility for relief rests with localities now, as ever, yet the Federal Government has always had and still has a continuing responsibility for the broader public welfare. It will soon fulfill that responsibility. . . .

One word more: Out of every crisis, every tribulation, every disaster, mankind rises with some share of greater knowledge, of higher decency, of purer purpose. Today we shall have come through a period of loose thinking, descending morals, an era of selfishness, of individual men and women and of whole nations. Blame not governments alone for this. Blame ourselves in equal share. Let us be frank in acknowledgment of the truth that many amongst us have made obeisance to Mammon, that the profits of speculation, the easy road without toil, have lured us from the old barricades. To return to higher standards we must abandon the false prophets and seek new leaders of our own choosing.

Never before, never before in modern history have the essential differences between the two major American parties stood out in such striking contrast as they do today. Republican leaders not only have failed in material things, they have failed in National vision, because in disaster they have held out no hope, they have pointed out no path for the people below to climb back to places of security and of safety in our American life.

Throughout the nation, men and women, forgotten in the political philosophy of the government of the last years look to us here for guidance and for more equitable opportunity to share in the distribution of national wealth.

On the farms, in the large metropolitan areas, in the smaller cities and in the villages, millions of our citizens cherish the hope that their old standards of living and of thought have not gone forever. Those millions cannot and shall not hope in vain.

I pledge you—I pledge myself to a new deal for the American people. Let us all here assembled constitute ourselves prophets of a new order of competence and of courage. This is more than a political campaign; it is a call to arms. Give me your help, not to win votes alone, but to win in this crusade to restore America to its own people.

Commonwealth Club of San Francisco
September 23, 1932

During his first presidential campaign, Roosevelt addressed the
Commonwealth Club of San Francisco on September 23, 1932.
Avoiding on this occasion any reference to partisan politics—
Roosevelt nowhere in this speech mentions his opponent Herbert
Hoover or the fact that he himself is running for president—FDR
took this opportunity to make a broad, sweeping statement of his
personal political philosophy. He positioned his ideas and outlook
in terms of historical American traditions established by Thomas
Jefferson and by FDR's two great personal mentors, Woodrow
Wilson and Theodore Roosevelt. TR's signal phrase—his reference to "malefactors of great wealth"—resonated powerfully with
FDR throughout his political life. During the early years of the
New Deal, when Roosevelt returned again and again to the idea
of protection for the common man against the power of unprin-
cipled special interests, he was carrying forward the legacy of his
distinguished cousin and predecessor.

I count it a privilege to be invited to address the Commonwealth Club.
It has stood in the life of this city and state, and it is perhaps accurate
to add, the nation, as a group of citizen leaders interested in fundamental problems of government, and chiefly concerned with achievement of progress in government through non-partisan means. The
privilege of addressing you, therefore, in the heat of a political campaign, is great. I want to respond to your courtesy in terms consistent
with your policy.

I want to speak not of politics but of government. I want to speak not
of parties, but of universal principles. They are not political, except in
that larger sense in which a great American once expressed a definition
of politics, that nothing in all of human life is foreign to the science of
politics. . . .

The issue of government has always been whether individual men and women will have to serve some system of government or economics, or whether a system of government and economics exists to serve individual men and women. This question has persistently dominated the discussion of government for many generations. On questions relating to these things men have differed, and for time immemorial it is probable that honest men will continue to differ.

The final word belongs to no man; yet we can still believe in change and in progress. Democracy, as a dear old friend of mine in Indiana, Meredith Nicholson, has called it, is a quest, a never-ending seeking for better things, and in the seeking for these things and the striving for them, there are many roads to follow. But, if we map the course of these roads, we find that there are only two general directions.

When we look about us, we are likely to forget how hard people have worked to win the privilege of government. The growth of the national governments of Europe was a struggle for the development of a centralized force in the nation, strong enough to impose peace upon ruling barons. In many instances the victory of the central government, the creation of a strong central government, was a haven of refuge to the individual. The people preferred the master far away to the exploitation and cruelty of the smaller master near at hand.

But the creators of national government were perforce ruthless men. They were often cruel in their methods, but they did strive steadily toward something that society needed and very much wanted, a strong central state, able to keep the peace, to stamp out civil war, to put the unruly nobleman in his place, and to permit the bulk of individuals to live safely. The man of ruthless force had his place in developing a pioneer country, just as he did in fixing the power of the central government in the development of nations. Society paid him well for his services and its development. When the development among the nations of Europe, however, had been completed, ambition and ruthlessness, having served its term, tended to overstep its mark.

There came a growing feeling that government was conducted for the benefit of a few who thrived unduly at the expense of all. The people sought a balancing—a limiting force. There came gradually, through town councils, trade guilds, national parliaments, by constitution and by popular participation and control, limitations on arbitrary power.

Another factor that tended to limit the power of those who ruled, was the rise of the ethical conception that a ruler bore a responsibility for the welfare of his subjects.

The American colonies were born in this struggle. The American Revolution was a turning point in it. After the revolution the struggle continued and shaped itself in the public life of the country. There were those who because they had seen the confusion which attended the years of war for American independence surrendered to the belief that popular government was essentially dangerous and essentially unworkable. They were honest people, my friends, and we cannot deny that their experience had warranted some measure of fear. The most brilliant, honest and able exponent of this point of view was Hamilton. He was too impatient of slow-moving methods. Fundamentally he believed that the safety of the republic lay in the autocratic strength of its government, that the destiny of individuals was to serve that government, and that fundamentally a great and strong group of central institutions, guided by a small group of able and public spirited citizens could best direct all government.

But Mr. Jefferson, in the summer of 1776, after drafting the Declaration of Independence turned his mind to the same problem and took a different view. He did not deceive himself with outward forms. Government to him was a means to an end, not an end in itself; it might be either a refuge and a help or a threat and a danger, depending on the circumstances. We find him carefully analyzing the society for which he was to organize a government. "We have no paupers. The great mass of our population is of laborers, our rich who cannot live without labor, either manual or professional, being few and of moderate wealth. Most of the laboring class possess property, cultivate their own lands, have families and from the demand for their labor, are enabled to exact from the rich and the competent such prices as enable them to feed abundantly, clothe above mere decency, to labor moderately and raise their families."

These people, he considered, had two sets of rights, those of "personal competency" and those involved in acquiring and possessing property. By "personal competency" he meant the right of free thinking, freedom of forming and expressing opinions, and freedom of personal living each man according to his own lights. To insure the first set of rights, a government must so order its functions as not to interfere with the individual. But even Jefferson realized that the exercise of the property rights might so interfere with the rights of the individual that the government, without whose assistance the property rights could not exist, must intervene, not to destroy individualism but to protect it.

You are familiar with the great political duel which followed; and how Hamilton, and his friends, building towards a dominant centralized power were at length defeated in the great election of 1800, by Mr. Jefferson's party. Out of that duel came the two parties, Republican and Democratic, as we know them today.

So began, in American political life, the new day, the day of the individual against the system, the day in which individualism was made the great watchword of American life. The happiest of economic conditions made that day long and splendid. On the Western frontier, land was substantially free. No one, who did not shirk the task of earning a living, was entirely without opportunity to do so. Depressions could, and did, come and go; but they could not alter the fundamental fact that most of the people lived partly by selling their labor and partly by extracting their livelihood from the soil, so that starvation and dislocation were practically impossible. At the very worst there was always the possibility of climbing into a covered wagon and moving west where the untilled prairies afforded a haven for men to whom the East did not provide a place. So great were our natural resources that we could offer this relief not only to our own people, but to the distressed of all the world; we could invite immigration from Europe, and welcome it with open arms. Traditionally, when a depression came a new section of land was opened in the West; and even our temporary misfortune served our manifest destiny.

It was in the middle of the 19th century that a new force was released and a new dream created. The force was what is called the industrial revolution, the advance of steam and machinery and the rise of the forerunners of the modern industrial plant. The dream was the dream of an economic machine, able to raise the standard of living for everyone; to bring luxury within the reach of the humblest; to annihilate distance by steam power and later by electricity, and to release everyone from the drudgery of the heaviest manual toil. It was to be expected that this would necessarily affect government. Heretofore, government had merely been called upon to produce conditions within which people could live happily, labor peacefully, and rest secure. Now it was called upon to aid in the consummation of this new dream. There was, however, a shadow over the dream. To be made real, it required use of the talents of men of tremendous will, and tremendous ambition, since by no other force could the problems of financing and engineering and new developments be brought to a consummation.

So manifest were the advantages of the machine age, however, that the United States fearlessly, cheerfully, and, I think, rightly, accepted the bitter with the sweet. It was thought that no price was too high to pay for the advantages which we could draw from a finished industrial system. The history of the last half century is accordingly in large measure a history of a group of financial Titans, whose methods were not scrutinized with too much care, and who were honored in proportion as they produced the results, irrespective of the means they used. The financiers who pushed the railroads to the Pacific were always ruthless, often wasteful, and frequently corrupt; but they did build railroads, and we have them today. It has been estimated that the American investor paid for the American railway system more than three times over in the process; but despite this fact the net advantage was to the United States. As long as we had free land; as long as population was growing by leaps and bounds; as long as our industrial plants were insufficient to supply our own needs, society chose to give the ambitious man free play and unlimited reward provided only that he produced the economic plant so much desired.

During this period of expansion, there was equal opportunity for all and the business of government was not to interfere but to assist in the development of industry. This was done at the request of business men themselves. The tariff was originally imposed for the purpose of "fostering our infant industry," a phrase I think the older among you will remember as a political issue not so long ago. The railroads were subsidized, sometimes by grants of money, oftener by grants of land; some of the most valuable oil lands in the United States were granted to assist the financing of the railroad which pushed through the Southwest. A nascent merchant marine was assisted by grants of money, or by mail subsidies, so that our steam shipping might ply the seven seas. Some of my friends tell me that they do not want the Government in business. With this I agree; but I wonder whether they realize the implications of the past. For while it has been American doctrine that the government must not go into business in competition with private enterprises, still it has been traditional particularly in Republican administrations for business urgently to ask the government to put at private disposal all kinds of government assistance. The same man who tells you that he does not want to see the government interfere in business—and he means it, and has plenty of good reasons for saying so—is the first to go to Washington and ask the government for a prohibitory tariff on his product. When things get just bad enough—as they did two years ago—he will go with equal speed to the United States government and ask for a loan; and the Reconstruction Finance Corporation is the outcome of it. Each group has sought protection from the government for its own special interests, without realizing that the function of government must be to favor no small group at the expense of its duty to protect the rights of personal freedom and of private property of all its citizens.

In retrospect we can now see that the turn of the tide came with the turn of the century. We were reaching our last frontier; there was no more free land and our industrial combinations had become great uncontrolled and irresponsible units of power within the state. Clearsighted men saw with fear the danger that opportunity would no longer be equal; that the growing corporation, like the feudal baron of old, might threaten the economic freedom of individuals to earn a living. In that hour, our antitrust laws were born. The cry was raised against the great corporations. Theodore Roosevelt, the first great Republican progressive, fought a Presidential campaign on the issue of "trust busting" and talked freely about malefactors of great wealth. If the government had a policy it was rather to turn the clock back, to destroy the large combinations and to return to the time when every man owned his individual small business.

This was impossible; Theodore Roosevelt, abandoning the idea of "trust busting," was forced to work out a difference between "good" trusts and "bad" trusts. The Supreme Court set forth the famous "rule of reason" by which it seems to have meant that a concentration of industrial power was permissible if the method by which it got its power, and the use it made of that power, was reasonable.

Woodrow Wilson, elected in 1912, saw the situation more clearly. Where Jefferson had feared the encroachment of political power on the lives of individuals, Wilson knew that the new power was financial. He saw, in the highly centralized economic system, the despot of the twentieth century, on whom great masses of individuals relied for their safety and their livelihood, and whose irresponsibility and greed (if it were not controlled) would reduce them to starvation and penury. The concentration of financial power had not proceeded so far in 1912 as it has today; but it had grown far enough for Mr. Wilson to realize fully its implications. It is interesting, now, to read his speeches. What is called "radical" today (and I have reason to know whereof I speak) is mild compared to the campaign of Mr. Wilson. "No man can deny," he said, "that the lines of endeavor have more and more narrowed and stiffened; no man who knows anything about the development of industry in this country can have failed to observe that the larger kinds of credit are more and more difficult to obtain unless you obtain them upon terms of uniting your efforts with those who already control the industry of the country, and nobody can fail to observe that every man who tries to set himself up in competition with any process of manufacture which has taken place under the control of large combinations of capital will presently find himself either squeezed out or obliged to sell and allow himself to be absorbed." Had there been no World War—had Mr. Wilson been able to devote eight years to domestic instead of to international affairs—we might have had a wholly different situation at the present time. However, the then distant roar of European cannon, growing ever louder, forced him to abandon the study of this issue. The problem he saw so clearly is left with us as a legacy; and no one of us on either side of the political controversy can deny that it is a matter of grave concern to the government.

A glance at the situation today only too clearly indicates that equality of opportunity as we have known it no longer exists. Our industrial plant is built; the problem just now is whether under existing conditions it is not overbuilt. Our last frontier has long since been reached, and there is practically no more free land. More than half of our people do not live on the farms or on lands and cannot derive a living by cultivating their own property. There is no safety valve in the form of a Western prairie to which those thrown out of work by the Eastern economic machines can go for a new start. We are not able to invite the immigration from Europe to share our endless plenty. We are now providing a drab living for our own people.

Our system of constantly rising tariffs has at last reacted against us to the point of closing our Canadian frontier on the north, our European markets on the east, many of our Latin American markets to the south, and a goodly proportion of our Pacific markets on the west, through the retaliatory tariffs of those countries. It has forced many of our great industrial institutions who exported their surplus production to such countries, to establish plants in such countries, within the tariff walls. This has resulted in the reduction of the operation of their American plants, and opportunity for employment.

Just as freedom to farm has ceased, so also the opportunity in business has narrowed. It still is true that men can start small enterprises, trusting to native shrewdness and ability to keep abreast of competitors; but area after area has been preempted altogether by the great corporations, and even in the fields which still have no great concerns, the small man starts under a handicap. The unfeeling statistics of the past three decades show that the independent business man is running a losing race. Perhaps he is forced to the wall; perhaps he cannot command credit; perhaps he is "squeezed out," in Mr. Wilson's words, by highly organized corporate competitors, as your corner grocery man can tell you. Recently a careful study was made of the concentration of business in the United States. It showed that our economic life was dominated by some six hundred odd corporations who controlled two-thirds of American industry. Ten million small business men divided the other third. More striking still, it appeared that if the process of concentration goes on at the same rate, at the end of another century we shall have all American industry controlled by a dozen corporations, and run by perhaps a hundred men. Put plainly, we are steering a steady course toward economic oligarchy, if we are not there already.

Clearly, all this calls for a re-appraisal of values. A mere builder of more industrial plants, a creator of more railroad systems, an organizer of more corporations, is as likely to be a danger as a help. The day of the great promoter or the financial Titan, to whom we granted anything if only he would build, or develop, is over. Our task now is not discovery or exploitation of natural resources, or necessarily producing more goods. It is the soberer, less dramatic business of administering resources and plants already in hand, of seeking to reestablish foreign markets for our surplus production, of meeting the problem of under-consumption, of adjusting production to consumption, of distributing wealth and products more equitably, of adapting existing economic organizations to the service of the people. The day of enlightened administration has come.

Just as in older times the central government was first a haven of refuge, and then a threat, so now in a closer economic system the central and ambitious financial unit is no longer a servant of national desire, but a danger. I would draw the parallel one step farther. We did not think because national government had become a threat in the 18th century that therefore we should abandon the principle of national government. Nor today should we abandon the principle of strong economic units called corporations, merely because their power is susceptible of easy abuse. In other times we dealt with the problem of an unduly ambitious central government by modifying it gradually into a constitutional democratic government. So today we are modifying and controlling our economic units.

As I see it, the task of government in its relation to business is to assist the development of an economic declaration of rights, an economic constitutional order. This is the common task of statesman and business man. It is the minimum requirement of a more permanently safe order of things. . . .

Every man has a right to life; and this means that he has also a right to make a comfortable living. He may by sloth or crime decline to exercise that right; but it may not be denied him. We have no actual famine or dearth; our industrial and agricultural mechanism can produce enough and to spare. Our government formal and informal, political and economic, owes to every one an avenue to possess himself of a portion of that plenty sufficient for his needs, through his own work.

Every man has a right to his own property; which means a right to be assured, to the fullest extent attainable, in the safety of his savings. By no other means can men carry the burdens of those parts of life which, in the nature of things, afford no chance of labor; childhood, sickness, old age. In all thought of property, this right is paramount; all other property rights must yield to it. If, in accord with this principle, we must restrict the operations of the speculator, the manipulator, even the financier, I believe we must accept the restriction as needful, not to hamper individualism but to protect it.

These two requirements must be satisfied, in the main, by the individuals who claim and hold control of the great industrial and financial combinations which dominate so large a part of our industrial life. They have undertaken to be, not business men, but princes—princes of property. I am not prepared to say that the system which produces them is wrong. I am very clear that they must fearlessly and competently assume the responsibility which goes with the power. So many enlightened business men know this that the statement would be little more than a platitude, were it not for an added implication.

This implication is, briefly, that the responsible heads of finance and industry instead of acting each for himself, must work together to achieve the common end. They must, where necessary, sacrifice this or that private advantage; and in reciprocal self-denial must seek a general advantage. It is here that formal government—political government, if you choose, comes in. Whenever in the pursuit of this objective the lone wolf, the unethical competitor, the reckless promoter, the Ishmael or Insull whose hand is against every man's, declines to join in achieving an end recognized as being for the public welfare, and threatens to drag the industry back to a state of anarchy, the government may properly be asked to apply restraint. Likewise, should the group ever use its collective power contrary to the public welfare, the government must be swift to enter and protect the public interest.

The government should assume the function of economic regulation only as a last resort, to be tried only when private initiative, inspired by high responsibility, with such assistance and balance as government can give, has finally failed. As yet there has been no final failure, because there has been no attempt; and I decline to assume that this nation is unable to meet the situation.

The final term of the high contract was for liberty and the pursuit of happiness. We have learnt a great deal of both in the past century. We know that individual liberty and individual happiness mean nothing unless both are ordered in the sense that one man's meat is not another man's poison. We know that the old "rights of personal competency"— the right to read, to think, to speak, to choose and live a mode of life, must be respected at all hazards. We know that liberty to do anything which deprives others of those elemental rights is outside the protection of any compact; and that government in this regard is the maintenance of a balance, within which every individual may have a place if he will take it; in which every individual may find safety if he wishes it; in which every individual may attain such power as his ability permits, consistent with his assuming the accompanying responsibility. . . .

Faith in America, faith in our tradition of personal responsibility, faith in our institutions, faith in ourselves demands that we recognize the new terms of the old social contract. We shall fulfill them, as we fulfilled the obligation of the apparent Utopia which Jefferson imagined for us in 1776, and which Jefferson, Roosevelt and Wilson sought to bring to realization. We must do so, lest a rising tide of misery engendered by our common failure, engulf us all. But failure is not an American habit; and in the strength of great hope we must all shoulder our common load.

First Inaugural Address
Washington, D.C., March 4, 1933

If Roosevelt knew one thing in 1932, it was his New Deal program had to be sold to the American public. He campaigned hard, traveling over 12,000 miles to every section of the country and giving over 200 speeches. The electorate responded. He won the presidency by 57.4% of the popular vote to 39.7% for the incumbent Herbert Hoover. The vote in the electoral college was 472 to 59 with FDR winning forty-two of the forty-eight states. His inauguration as the thirty-second president was set for Saturday, March 4, 1933. The most dramatic incident in the months leading up to the inauguration was an assassination attempt at virtually point-blank range following a brief speech at Miami's Bay Front Park in February. Miraculously, the president-elect escaped unscathed, and from all accounts supremely untroubled; but the attack did take the life of another prominent Democrat, Mayor Anton Cermak of Chicago. Roosevelt's advisors took pains to reassure the nation that the incident was not part of a political plot to stifle the New Deal before it was launched—just the act of a single gunman driven by illness and personal demons. In due course, the perpetrator—who was captured at the scene—was tried, convicted and executed.

Economic conditions had worsened during the long Depression winter between the November election and the March inauguration. The most immediate problem confronting FDR as he took office concerned the banking system. Banks everywhere had failed, confidence in the nation's banking system was eroding, and depositors large and small worried about the safety of their funds. In a situation where panic tended to feed on itself, runs on banks intensified as people decided to hoard what gold and currency they had. The entire banking system was in free fall as inauguration Saturday approached, with the governors of many states having issued proclamations shutting down banks over which they had control. The gravity of the situation was

28

brought home to many visitors to Washington who had come to celebrate the inauguration when hotels there refused out-of-town checks, and wires for cash from home were limited to $100 because of the currency shortage. It was later reported that Eleanor Roosevelt had wondered how in these circumstances the large Roosevelt entourage would be able to pay for their accommodations at the Mayflower Hotel which, of course, included the presidential suite. After a few days, the major hotels realized it would benefit no one to keep their guests captive because they couldn't pay with local checks, and most of them relented.

With the Navy airship *Akron* circling overhead and a crowd of 100,000 in attendance in front of the east portico of the Capitol, Roosevelt took the oath of office from Chief Justice Charles Evans Hughes. FDR's hand was on an old Dutch Bible which had been used by his family to record births and deaths for over 200 years, open to his favorite passage in Paul's First Epistle to the Corinthians: "And now abideth Faith, Hope, Charity, these three, but the greatest of these is Charity." Addressing the banking situation, Roosevelt outlined his plans only in the most general terms—except for announcing that he was about to call a special session of Congress because of the crisis at hand. "The only thing we have to fear is fear itself," was his memorable pronouncement in the opening segment of this first inaugural address. Eleanor Roosevelt told a reporter how she perceived the event a few days later: "It was very, very solemn," she said. "And a little terrifying." At one o'clock in the morning on Monday, March 6th—thirty-six hours into the new presidency—the White House issued a proclamation, based on powers FDR's legal advisors found vested in the president under a "World War One Trading with the Enemy Act" still on the books. The proclamation declared that a national bank holiday would begin that day, absolutely suspending all banking transactions throughout the country. The legal underpinnings of this move may have been improvisational, but the crisis was so grave, and the efforts of the preceding administration to deal with it so futile, that objections were few.

I am certain that my fellow Americans expect that on my induction into the Presidency I will address them with a candor and a decision which the present situation of our Nation impels. This is preeminently the time to speak the truth, the whole truth, frankly and boldly. Nor need we shrink from honestly facing conditions in our country today. This great Nation will endure as it has endured, will revive and will prosper. So, first of all, let me assert my firm belief that the only thing we have to fear is fear itself—nameless, unreasoning, unjustified terror which paralyzes needed efforts to convert retreat into advance. In every dark hour of our national life a leadership of frankness and vigor has met with that understanding and support of the people themselves which is essential to victory. I am convinced that you will again give that support to leadership in these critical days.

In such a spirit on my part and on yours we face our common difficulties. They concern, thank God, only material things. Values have shrunken to fantastic levels; taxes have risen; our ability to pay has fallen; government of all kinds is faced by serious curtailment of income; the means of exchange are frozen in the currents of trade; the withered leaves of industrial enterprise lie on every side; farmers find no markets for their produce; the savings of many years in thousands of families are gone.

More important, a host of unemployed citizens face the grim problem of existence, and an equally great number toil with little return. Only a foolish optimist can deny the dark realities of the moment.

Yet our distress comes from no failure of substance. We are stricken by no plague of locusts. Compared with the perils which our forefathers conquered because they believed and were not afraid, we have still much to be thankful for. Nature still offers her bounty and human efforts have multiplied it. Plenty is at our doorstep, but a generous use of it languishes in the very sight of the supply. Primarily this is because the rulers of the exchange of mankind's goods have failed, through their own stubbornness and their own incompetence, have admitted their failure, and abdicated. Practices of the unscrupulous money changers stand indicted in the court of public opinion, rejected by the hearts and minds of men.

True they have tried, but their efforts have been cast in the pattern of an outworn tradition. Faced by failure of credit they have proposed only the lending of more money. Stripped of the lure of profit by which to induce our people to follow their false leadership, they have resorted to exhortations, pleading tearfully for restored confidence. They know only the rules of a generation of self-seekers. They have no vision, and when there is no vision the people perish.

The money changers have fled from their high seats in the temple of our civilization. We may now restore that temple to the ancient truths. The measure of the restoration lies in the extent to which we apply social values more noble than mere monetary profit.

Happiness lies not in the mere possession of money; it lies in the joy of achievement, in the thrill of creative effort. The joy and moral stimulation of work no longer must be forgotten in the mad chase of evanescent profits. These dark days will be worth all they cost us if they teach us that our true destiny is not to be ministered unto but to minister to ourselves and to our fellow men.

Recognition of the falsity of material wealth as the standard of success goes hand in hand with the abandonment of the false belief that public office and high political position are to be valued only by the standards of pride of place and personal profit; and there must be an end to a conduct in banking and in business which too often has given to a sacred trust the likeness of callous and selfish wrongdoing. Small wonder that confidence languishes, for it thrives only on honesty, on honor, on the sacredness of obligations, on faithful protection, on unselfish performance; without them it cannot live.

Restoration calls, however, not for changes in ethics alone. This Nation asks for action, and action now.

Our greatest primary task is to put people to work. This is no unsolvable problem if we face it wisely and courageously. It can be accomplished in part by direct recruiting by the Government itself, treating the task as we would treat the emergency of a war, but at the same time, through this employment, accomplishing greatly needed projects to stimulate and reorganize the use of our natural resources.

Hand in hand with this we must frankly recognize the overbalance of population in our industrial centers and, by engaging on a national scale in a redistribution, endeavor to provide a better use of the land for those best fitted for the land. The task can be helped by definite efforts to raise the values of agricultural products and with this the power to purchase the output of our cities. It can be helped by preventing realistically the tragedy of the growing loss through foreclosure of our small homes and our farms. It can be helped by insistence that the Federal, State, and local governments act forthwith on the demand that their cost be drastically reduced. It can be helped by the unifying of relief activities which today are often scattered, uneconomical, and unequal. It can be helped by national planning for and supervision of all forms of transportation and of communications and other utilities which have a definitely public character. There are many ways in which it can be helped, but it can never be helped merely by talking about it. We must act and act quickly.

Finally, in our progress toward a resumption of work we require two safeguards against a return of the evils of the old order; there must be a strict supervision of all banking and credits and investments; there must be an end to speculation with other people's money, and there must be provision for an adequate but sound currency.

These are the lines of attack. I shall presently urge upon a new Congress in special session detailed measures for their fulfillment, and I shall seek the immediate assistance of the several States.

Through this program of action we address ourselves to putting our own national house in order and making income balance outgo. Our international trade relations, though vastly important, are in point of time and necessity secondary to the establishment of a sound national economy. I favor as a practical policy the putting of first things first. I shall spare no effort to restore world trade by international economic readjustment, but the emergency at home cannot wait on that accomplishment.

The basic thought that guides these specific means of national recovery is not narrowly nationalistic. It is the insistence, as a first consideration, upon the interdependence of the various elements in all parts of the United States—a recognition of the old and permanently important manifestation of the American spirit of the pioneer. It is the way to recovery. It is the immediate way. It is the strongest assurance that the recovery will endure.

In the field of world policy I would dedicate this Nation to the policy of the good neighbor—the neighbor who resolutely respects himself and, because he does so, respects the rights of others—the neighbor who respects his obligations and respects the sanctity of his agreements in and with a world of neighbors.

If I read the temper of our people correctly, we now realize as we have never realized before our interdependence on each other; that we can not merely take but we must give as well; that if we are to go forward, we must move as a trained and loyal army willing to sacrifice for the good of a common discipline, because without such discipline no progress is made, no leadership becomes effective. We are, I know, ready and willing to submit our lives and property to such discipline, because it makes possible a leadership which aims at a larger good. This I propose to offer, pledging that the larger purposes will bind upon us all as a sacred obligation with a unity of duty hitherto evoked only in time of armed strife.

With this pledge taken, I assume unhesitatingly the leadership of this great army of our people dedicated to a disciplined attack upon our common problems.

Action in this image and to this end is feasible under the form of government which we have inherited from our ancestors. Our Constitution is so simple and practical that it is possible always to meet extraordinary needs by changes in emphasis and arrangement without loss of essential form. That is why our constitutional system has proved itself the most superbly enduring political mechanism the modern world has produced. It has met every stress of vast expansion of territory, of foreign wars, of bitter internal strife, of world relations.

It is to be hoped that the normal balance of executive and legislative authority may be wholly adequate to meet the unprecedented task before us. But it may be that an unprecedented demand and need for undelayed action may call for temporary departure from that normal balance of public procedure.

I am prepared under my constitutional duty to recommend the measures that a stricken nation in the midst of a stricken world may require. These measures, or such other measures as the Congress may build out of its experience and wisdom, I shall seek, within my constitutional authority, to bring to speedy adoption.

But in the event that the Congress shall fail to take one of these two courses, and in the event that the national emergency is still critical, I shall not evade the clear course of duty that will then confront me. I shall ask the Congress for the one remaining instrument to meet the crisis—broad Executive power to wage a war against the emergency, as great as the power that would be given to me if we were in fact invaded by a foreign foe.

For the trust reposed in me I will return the courage and the devotion that befit the time. I can do no less.

We face the arduous days that lie before us in the warm courage of the national unity; with the clear consciousness of seeking old and precious moral values; with the clean satisfaction that comes from the stern performance of duty by old and young alike. We aim at the assurance of a rounded and permanent national life.

We do not distrust the future of essential democracy. The people of the United States have not failed. In their need they have registered a mandate that they want direct, vigorous action. They have asked for discipline and direction under leadership. They have made me the present instrument of their wishes. In the spirit of the gift I take it.

In this dedication of a Nation we humbly ask the blessing of God. May He protect each and every one of us. May He guide me in the days to come.

First Fireside Chat
Washington, D.C., March 12, 1933

FDR brought something new to American political life at the end of his first week in office when, on Sunday, March 12, 1933, he delivered by radio from the White House's Diplomatic Reception Room, the first of his twenty-seven presidential Fireside Chats. The term "Fireside Chat" wasn't Roosevelt's own—it was first used by an executive of the Columbia Broadcasting System, Harry C. Butcher, at the time of the second one on May 7, 1933. But FDR had used the radio to address the public on political issues while governor of New York State, and he was fully aware of the potential of the medium for reaching a vast audience. The Fireside Chats became an important asset in the political arsenal of the New Deal's brain trust. Roosevelt and his advisors felt it allowed them to make their case directly to the people, instead of having their views and policies refracted through the lens of a frequently hostile press. Even more importantly, they enabled the New Dealers to take maximum advantage of FDR's superb communication skills. Usually speaking on a single issue for fifteen to thirty minutes, and often on Sunday evenings when people were at home and the expected audiences were largest, the Roosevelt of the Fireside Chats was typically optimistic, even buoyant. And his always convincing aura of informality successfully masked the fact that these speeches were meticulously prepared through many drafts and revisions to achieve the desired effect. Roosevelt delivered six Fireside Chats during the first nineteen months of the New Deal, then six more during the next four years. Fifteen more followed during World War II. It was often estimated that audiences of over 30 to 40 million people tuned in—out of a total population of 130 million—and these occasions always generated a huge response by mail and telegram.

The first Fireside Chat concerned the banking crisis, the special session of Congress which had been called in the week just past to deal with it, and the Emergency Banking Act which had been the result. Roosevelt outlined the government's actions intended to give the nation's banks some breathing space, and to separate solvent from insolvent banks. Most importantly, he gave details of the schedule under which sound banks would reopen the following week, and asked above all for calm. It worked. The nation's solvent banks reopened according to the progressive schedule outlined in the Fireside Chat, and after a few days it became apparent that deposits were outstripping withdrawals. The specter of unreasoning fear had been beaten back—at least temporarily.

I want to talk for a few minutes with the people of the United States about banking—with the comparatively few who understand the mechanics of banking but more particularly with the overwhelming majority who use banks for the making of deposits and the drawing of checks. I want to tell you what has been done in the last few days, why it was done, and what the next steps are going to be. I recognize that the many proclamations from State Capitols and from Washington, the legislation, the Treasury regulations, etc., couched for the most part in banking and legal terms should be explained for the benefit of the average citizen. I owe this in particular because of the fortitude and good temper with which everybody has accepted the inconvenience and hardships of the banking holiday. I know that when you understand what we in Washington have been about I shall continue to have your cooperation as fully as I have had your sympathy and help during the past week.

First of all let me state the simple fact that when you deposit money in a bank the bank does not put the money into a safe deposit vault. It invests your money in many different forms of credit-bonds, commercial paper, mortgages and many other kinds of loans. In other words, the bank puts your money to work to keep the wheels of industry and of agriculture turning around. A comparatively small part of the money you put into the bank is kept in currency—an amount which in normal times is wholly sufficient to cover the cash needs of the average citizen. In other words the total amount of all the currency in the country is only a small fraction of the total deposits in all of the banks.

What, then, happened during the last few days of February and the first few days of March? Because of undermined confidence on the part of the public, there was a general rush by a large portion of our population to turn bank deposits into currency or gold.—A rush so great that the soundest banks could not get enough currency to meet the demand. The reason for this was that on the spur of the moment it was, of course, impossible to sell perfectly sound assets of a bank and convert them into cash except at panic prices far below the real value.

By the afternoon of March 3 scarcely a bank in the country was open to do business. Proclamations temporarily closing them in whole or in part had been issued by the Governors in almost all the states.

It was then that I issued the proclamation providing for the nation-wide bank holiday, and this was the first step in the Government's reconstruction of our financial and economic fabric.

The second step was the legislation promptly and patriotically passed by the Congress confirming my proclamation and broadening my powers so that it became possible in view of the requirement of time to entend [sic] the holiday and lift the ban of that holiday gradually. This law also gave authority to develop a program of rehabilitation of our banking facilities. I want to tell our citizens in every part of the Nation that the national Congress—Republicans and Democrats alike—showed by this action a devotion to public welfare and a realization of the emergency and the necessity for speed that it is difficult to match in our history.

The third stage has been the series of regulations permitting the banks to continue their functions to take care of the distribution of food and household necessities and the payment of payrolls.

This bank holiday while resulting in many cases in great inconvenience is affording us the opportunity to supply the currency necessary to meet the situation. No sound bank is a dollar worse off than it was when it closed its doors last Monday. Neither is any bank which may turn out not to be in a position for immediate opening. The new law allows the twelve Federal Reserve banks to issue additional currency on good assets and thus the banks which reopen will be able to meet every legitimate call. The new currency is being sent out by the Bureau of Engraving and Printing in large volume to every part of the country. It is sound currency because it is backed by actual, good assets.

As a result we start tomorrow, Monday, with the opening of banks in the twelve Federal Reserve bank cities—those banks which on first examination by the Treasury have already been found to be all right. This will be followed on Tuesday by the resumption of all their functions by banks already found to be sound in cities where there are recognized clearing houses. That means about 250 cities of the United States.

On Wednesday and succeeding days banks in smaller places all through the country will resume business, subject, of course, to the Government's physical ability to complete its survey. It is necessary that the reopening of banks be extended over a period in order to permit the banks to make applications for necessary loans, to obtain currency needed to meet their requirements and to enable the Government to make common sense checkups. Let me make it clear to you that if your bank does not open the first day you are by no means justified in believing that it will not open. A bank that opens on one of the subsequent days is in exactly the same status as the bank that opens tomorrow.

I know that many people are worrying about State banks not members of the Federal Reserve System. These banks can and will receive assistance from members banks and from the Reconstruction Finance Corporation. These state banks are following the same course as the national banks except that they get their licenses to resume business from the state authorities, and these authorities have been asked by the Secretary of the Treasury to permit their good banks to open up on the same schedule as the national banks. I am confident that the state banking departments will be as careful as the National Government in the policy relating to the opening of banks and will follow the same broad policy. It is possible that when the banks resume a very few people who have not recovered from their fear may again begin withdrawals. Let me make it clear that the banks will take care of all needs—and it is my belief that hoarding during the past week has become an exceedingly unfashionable pastime. It needs no prophet to tell you that when the people find that they can get their money—that they can get it when they want it for all legitimate purposes—the phantom of fear will soon be laid. People will again be glad to have their money where it will be safely taken care of and where they can use it conveniently at any time. I can assure you that it is safer to keep your money in a reopened bank that under the mattress.

The success of our whole great national program depends, of course, upon the cooperation of the public—on its intelligent support and use of a reliable system.

Remember that the essential accomplishment of the new legislation is that it makes it possible for banks more readily to convert their assets into cash than was the case before. More liberal provision has been made for banks to borrow on these assets at the Reserve Banks and more liberal provision has also been made for issuing currency on the security of those good assets. This currency is not fiat currency. It is issued only on adequate security—and every good bank has an abundance of such security.

One more point before I close. There will be, of course, some banks unable to reopen without being reorganized. The new law allows the Government to assist in making these reorganizations quickly and effectively and even allows the Government to subscribe to at least a part of new capital which may be required.

I hope you can see from this elemental recital of what your government is doing that there is nothing complex, or radical in the process.

We had a bad banking situation. Some of our bankers had shown themselves either incompetent or dishonest in their handling of the people's funds. They had used the money entrusted to them in speculations and unwise loans. This was of course not true in the vast majority of our banks but it was true in enough of them to shock the people for a time into a sense of insecurity and to put them into a frame of mind where they did not differentiate, but seemed to assume that the acts of a comparative few had tainted them all. It was the Government's job to straighten out this situation and do it as quickly as possible—and the job is being performed.

I do not promise you that every bank will be reopened or that individual losses will not be suffered, but there will be no losses that possibly could be avoided; and there would have been more and greater losses had we continued to drift. I can even promise you salvation for some at least of the sorely pressed banks. We shall be engaged not merely in reopening sound banks but in the creation of sound banks through reorganization. It has been wonderful to me to catch the note of confidence from all over the country. I can never be sufficiently grateful to the people for the loyal support they have given me in their acceptance of the judgment that has dictated our course, even though all of our processes may not have seemed clear to them.

After all there is an element in the readjustment of our financial system more important than currency, more important than gold, and that is the confidence of the people. Confidence and courage are the essentials of success in carrying out our plan. You people must have faith; you must not be stampeded by rumors or guesses. Let us unite in banishing fear. We have provided the machinery to restore our financial system; it is up to you to support and make it work.

It is your problem no less than it is mine. Together we cannot fail.

Second Fireside Chat

Washington, D.C., May 7, 1933

FDR's first Fireside Chat, a week into his first administration, had focused exclusively on the banking crisis and the steps he was taking to deal with it. Two months later, Roosevelt took to the radio for the second time, this time to discuss more comprehensively the economic program of the New Deal. Urgent as the banking crisis was, the Depression—now in its fourth year—had many more facets. Industrial output was half of the pre-1929 level. A quarter of the American labor force, 13 to 15 million workers, were unemployed. Hourly wages were down 60% from their 1929 levels. White collar salaries were off nearly as much. The basic philosophy behind the New Deal was the idea that the unfettered operation of free market forces had created legions of forgotten economic casualties in America and around the world; that in addition to the forces generated by the marketplace, economic progress and security for everyone required much more comprehensive planning by the government than ever before, as well as cooperation—hopefully voluntary, but legislated if necessary, among various elements on the economic scene. Again and again in his speeches during this period, FDR emphasized the same point: 90% of the leaders in any industry might be reasonable, fair-minded people, but if just 10% paid unfairly low wages, or demanded unjustly long hours, the actions of those 10% would either force everyone else to do the same or go out of business because they couldn't compete. Roosevelt was committed to the idea that planning, persuasion, and legislation by the government could help everyone avoid the abuses of the past and move ahead into a new economic era.

In the first three months of the New Deal—the famous 100 days from FDR's inauguration—measure after measure was sent to Congress and passed into law. Prohibition was repealed, aid to the unemployed was increased, supports for failing crop prices were enacted, the Tennessee Valley Authority began the work of bringing electrical power to a vast underdeveloped portion of the country, the Civilian Conservation Corps started employing thousands of young men to plant trees and do other conservation work, the Public Works Administration began financing important civil building projects to stimulate economic growth and provide jobs, the powers of the already established Reconstruction Finance Corporation were broadened so that it could make loans to both large and small businesses. These and other programs were bold, imaginative initiatives which brought immediate help to many, but Roosevelt probably had no idea how right he was in that moment in May, 1933 when he said, "We can't bally-hoo ourselves back to prosperity." Despite the many laws enacted and new federal agencies created, the attempts to regulate economic activity, allocate resources productively and stimulate economic growth, the stagnant conditions of the Depression proved largely intractable through the remaining long years of the 1930s. Only the war and the huge demands it placed on the country's productivity finally ushered in a new era of widespread prosperity.

On a Sunday night a week after my Inauguration I used the radio to tell you about the banking crisis and the measures we were taking to meet it. I think that in that way I made clear to the country various facts that might otherwise have been misunderstood and in general provided a means of understanding which did much to restore confidence.

Tonight, eight weeks later, I come for the second time to give you my report—in the same spirit and by the same means to tell you about what we have been doing and what we are planning to do.

Two months ago we were facing serious problems. The country was dying by inches. It was dying because trade and commerce had declined to dangerously low levels; prices for basic commodities were such as to destroy the value of the assets of national institutions such as banks, savings banks, insurance companies, and others. These institutions, because of their great needs, were foreclosing mortgages, calling loans, refusing credit. Thus there was actually in process of destruction the property of millions of people who had borrowed money on that property in terms of dollars which had had an entirely different value from the level of March, 1933. That situation in that crisis did not call for any complicated consideration of economic panaceas or fancy plans. We were faced by a condition and not a theory.

There were just two alternatives: The first was to allow the foreclosures to continue, credit to be withheld and money to go into hiding, and thus forcing liquidation and bankruptcy of banks, railroads and insurance companies and a recapitalizing of all business and all property on a lower level. This alternative meant a continuation of what is loosely called "deflation," the net result of which would have been extraordinary hardship on all property owners and, incidentally, extraordinary hardships on all persons working for wages through an increase in unemployment and a further reduction of the wage scale.

It is easy to see that the result of this course would have not only economic effects of a very serious nature but social results that might bring incalculable harm. Even before I was inaugurated I came to the conclusion that such a policy was too much to ask the American people to bear. It involved not only a further loss of homes, farms, savings and wages but also a loss of spiritual values—the loss of that sense of security for the present and the future so necessary to the peace and contentment of the individual and of his family. When you destroy these things you will find it difficult to establish confidence of any sort in the future. It was clear that mere appeals from Washington for confidence and the mere lending of more money to shaky institutions could not stop this downward course. A prompt program applied as quickly as possible seemed to me not only justified but imperative to our national security. The Congress, and when I say Congress I mean the members of both political parties, fully understood this and gave me generous and intelligent support. The members of Congress realized that the methods of normal times had to be replaced in the emergency by measures which were suited to the serious and pressing requirements of the moment. There was no actual surrender of power, Congress still retained its constitutional authority and no one has the slightest desire to change the balance of these powers. The function of Congress is to decide what has to be done and to select the appropriate agency to carry out its will. This policy it has strictly adhered to. The only thing that has been happening has been to designate the President as the agency to carry out certain of the purposes of the Congress. This was constitutional and in keeping with the past American tradition.

The legislation which has been passed or in the process of enactment can properly be considered as part of a well-grounded plan.

First, we are giving opportunity of employment to one-quarter of a million of the unemployed, especially the young men who have dependents, to go into the forestry and flood prevention work. This is a big task because it means feeding, clothing and caring for nearly twice as many men as we have in the regular army itself. In creating this civilian conservation corps we are killing two birds with one stone. We are clearly enhancing the value of our natural resources and second, we are relieving an appreciable amount of actual distress. This great group of men have entered upon their work on a purely voluntary basis, no military training is involved and we are conserving not only our natural resources but our human resources. One of the great values to this work is the fact that it is direct and requires the intervention of very little machinery. Second, I have requested the Congress and have secured action upon a proposal to put the great properties owned by our Government at Muscle Shoals to work after long years of wasteful inaction, and with this a broad plan for the improvement of a vast area in the Tennessee Valley. It will add to the comfort and happiness of hundreds of thousands of people and the incident benefits will reach the entire nation.

Next, the Congress is about to pass legislation that will greatly ease the mortgage distress among the farmers and the home owners of the nation, by providing for the easing of the burden of debt now bearing so heavily upon millions of our people.

Our next step in seeking immediate relief is a grant of half a billion dollars to help the states, counties and municipalities in their duty to care for those who need direct and immediate relief.

The Congress also passed legislation authorizing the sale of beer in such states as desired. This has already resulted in considerable reemployment and, incidentally, has provided much needed tax revenue.

We are planning to ask the Congress for legislation to enable the Government to undertake public works, thus stimulating directly and indirectly the employment of many others in well-considered projects.

Further legislation has been taken up which goes much more fundamentally into our economic problems. The Farm Relief Bill seeks by the use of several methods, alone or together, to bring about an increased return to farmers for their major farm products, seeking at the same time to prevent in the days to come disastrous over-production which so often in the past has kept farm commodity prices far below a reasonable return. This measure provides wide powers for emergencies. The extent of its use will depend entirely upon what the future has in store.

Well-considered and conservative measures will likewise be proposed which will attempt to give to the industrial workers of the country a more fair wage return, prevent cut-throat competition and unduly long hours for labor, and at the same time to encourage each industry to prevent over-production.

Our Railroad Bill falls into the same class because it seeks to provide and make certain definite planning by the railroads themselves, with the assistance of the Government, to eliminate the duplication and waste that is now resulting in railroad receiverships and continuing operating deficits. I am certain that the people of this country understand and approve the broad purposes behind these new governmental policies relating to agriculture and industry and transportation. We found ourselves faced with more agricultural products than we could possibly consume ourselves and surpluses which other nations did not have the cash to buy from us except at prices ruinously low. We have found our factories able to turn out more goods than we could possibly consume, and at the same time we were faced with a falling export demand. We found ourselves with more facilities to transport goods and crops than there were goods and crops to be transported. All of this has been caused in large part by a complete lack of planning and a complete failure to understand the danger signals that have been flying ever since the close of the World War. The people of this country have been erroneously encouraged to believe that they could keep on increasing the output of farm and factory indefinitely and that some magician would find ways and means for that increased output to be consumed with reasonable profit to the producer.

Today we have reason to believe that things are a little better than they were two months ago. Industry has picked up, railroads are carrying more freight, farm prices are better, but I am not going to indulge in issuing proclamations of overenthusiastic assurance. We cannot bally-ho ourselves back to prosperity. I am going to be honest at all times with the people of the country. I do not want the people of this country to take the foolish course of letting this improvement come back on another speculative wave. I do not want the people to believe that because of unjustified optimism we can resume the ruinous practice of increasing our crop output and our factory output in the hope that a kind providence will find buyers at high prices. Such a course may bring us immediate and false prosperity but it will be the kind of prosperity that will lead us into another tailspin. It is wholly wrong to call the measure that we have taken Government control of farming, control of industry, and control of transportation. It is rather a partnership between Government and farming and industry and transportation, not partnership in profits, for the profits would still go to the citizens, but rather a partnership in planning and partnership to see that the plans are carried out.

Let me illustrate with an example. Take the cotton goods industry. It is probably true that ninety per cent of the cotton manufacturers would agree to eliminate starvation wages, would agree to stop long hours of employment, would agree to stop child labor, would agree to prevent an overproduction that would result in unsalable surpluses. But, what good is such an agreement if the other ten per cent of cotton manufacturers pay starvation wages, require long hours, employ children in their mills and turn out burdensome surpluses? The unfair ten per cent could produce goods so cheaply that the fair ninety per cent would be compelled to meet the unfair conditions. Here is where government comes in. Government ought to have the right and will have the right, after surveying and planning for an industry to prevent, with the assistance of the overwhelming majority of that industry, unfair practice and to enforce this agreement by the authority of government. The so-called anti-trust laws were intended to prevent the creation of monopolies and to forbid unreasonable profits to those monopolies. That purpose of the anti-trust laws must be continued, but these laws were never intended to encourage the kind of unfair competition that results in long hours, starvation wages and overproduction.

The same principle applies to farm products and to transportation and every other field of organized private industry.

We are working toward a definite goal, which is to prevent the return of conditions which came very close to destroying what we call modern civilization. The actual accomplishment of our purpose cannot be attained in a day. Our policies are wholly within purposes for which our American Constitutional Government was established 150 years ago.

I know that the people of this country will understand this and will also understand the spirit in which we are undertaking this policy. I do not deny that we may make mistakes of procedure as we carry out the policy. I have no expectation of making a hit every time I come to bat. What I seek is the highest possible batting average, not only for myself but for the team. Theodore Roosevelt once said to me: "If I can be right 75 per cent of the time I shall come up to the fullest measure of my hopes."

Much has been said of late about Federal finances and inflation, the gold standard, etc. Let me make the facts very simple and my policy very clear. In the first place, government credit and government currency are really one and the same thing. Behind government bonds there is only a promise to pay. Behind government currency we have, in addition to the promise to pay, a reserve of gold and a small reserve of silver. In this connection it is worth while remembering that in the past the government has agreed to redeem nearly thirty billions of its debts and its currency in gold, and private corporations in this country have agreed to redeem another sixty or seventy billions of securities and mortgages in gold. The government and private corporations were making these agreements when they knew full well that all of the gold in the United States amounted to only between three and four billions and that all of the gold in all of the world amounted to only about eleven billions.

If the holders of these promises to pay started in to demand gold the first comers would get gold for a few days and they would amount to about one twenty-fifth of the holders of the securities and the currency. The other twenty-four people out of twenty-five, who did not happen to be at the top of the line, would be told politely that there was no more gold left. We have decided to treat all twenty-five in the same way in the interest of justice and the exercise of the constitutional powers of this government. We have placed every one on the same basis in order that the general good may be preserved.

Nevertheless, gold, and to a partial extent silver, are perfectly good bases for currency and that is why I decided not to let any of the gold now in the country go out of it.

A series of conditions arose three weeks ago which very readily might have meant, first, a drain on our gold by foreign countries, and secondly, as a result of that, a flight of American capital, in the form of gold, out of our country. It is not exaggerating the possibility to tell you that such an occurrence might well have taken from us the major part of our gold reserve and resulted in such a further weakening of our government and private credit as to bring on actual panic conditions and the complete stoppage of the wheels of industry.

The Administration has the definite objective of raising commodity prices to such an extent that those who have borrowed money will, on the average, be able to repay that money in the same kind of dollar which they borrowed. We do not seek to let them get such a cheap dollar that they will be able to pay back a great deal less than they borrowed. In other words, we seek to correct a wrong and not to create another wrong in the opposite direction. That is why powers are being given to the Administration to provide, if necessary, for an enlargement of credit, in order to correct the existing wrong. These powers will be used when, as, and if it may be necessary to accomplish the purpose.

Hand in hand with the domestic situation which, of course, is our first concern, is the world situation, and I want to emphasize to you that the domestic situation is inevitably and deeply tied in with the conditions in all of the other nations of the world. In other words, we can get, in all probability, a fair measure of prosperity return in the United States, but it will not be permanent unless we get a return to prosperity all over the world.

In the conferences which we have held and are holding with the leaders of other nations, we are seeking four great objectives. First, a general reduction of armaments and through this the removal of the fear of invasion and armed attack, and, at the same time, a reduction in armament costs, in order to help in the balancing of government budgets and the reduction of taxation. Secondly, a cutting down of the trade barriers, in order to re-start the flow of exchange of crops and goods between nations. Third, the setting up of a stabilization of currencies, in order that trade can make contracts ahead. Fourth, the reestablishment of friendly relations and greater confidence between all nations.

Our foreign visitors these past three weeks have responded to these purposes in a very helpful way. All of the Nations have suffered alike in this great depression. They have all reached the conclusion that each can best be helped by the common action of all. It is in this spirit that our visitors have met with us and discussed our common problems. The international conference that lies before us must succeed. The future of the world demands it and we have each of us pledged ourselves to the best joint efforts to this end.

To you, the people of this country, all of us, the Members of the Congress and the members of this Administration owe a profound debt of gratitude. Throughout the depression you have been patient. You have granted us wide powers, you have encouraged us with a widespread approval of our purposes. Every ounce of strength and every resource at our command we have devoted to the end of justifying your confidence. We are encouraged to believe that a wise and sensible beginning has been made. In the present spirit of mutual confidence and mutual encouragement we go forward.

Acceptance Speech
Philadelphia, June 27, 1936

In contrast to the political intrigue which led up to his first nomination for the presidency, in 1936 the incumbent FDR was renominated by acclamation of the Democratic party at their midsummer convention in Philadelphia. With the coming election against the popular Republican governor of Kansas, Alfred M. Landon, destined to be a referendum on the New Deal, FDR had two separate teams of speechwriters—Samuel Rosenman and Stanley High on one, Raymond Moley and Thomas Corcoran on the other—working independently on his acceptance speech. In the end, as he often did, FDR took material from both teams, opening with the more partisan and belligerent ideas of Rosenman and High, then switching to the more statesmanlike vision set forth by Moley and Corcoran. Toward the end came one of the most memorable passages FDR or any American president has ever uttered in public: "There is a mysterious cycle in human events. To some generations much is given. Of other generations much is expected. This generation of Americans has a rendezvous with destiny."

Some of the drama of that June night in Philadelphia was witnessed by only a small portion of the huge crowd in Franklin Field. Making his way laboriously to the podium with the assistance of his son James, FDR was jostled by a supporter and almost fell as one of his leg braces unsnapped. The Secret Service men nearby managed to break his fall, relock the brace, and gather up the pages of his forthcoming address. On the podium, FDR gave no hint of the mishap he had just suffered, delivering his fighting speech in powerful and confident tones; then, after circling the stadium twice in an open car, he set forth on the campaign that would in the end bring him the most one-sided victory of his presidency.

Senator Robinson, Members of the Democratic Convention, my friends:

Here and in every community throughout the land we are met at a time of great moment to the future of the Nation. It is an occasion to be dedicated to the simple and sincere expression of an attitude towards problems, the determination of which will profoundly affect America. . . .

But I cannot, with candor, tell you that all is well with the world. Clouds of suspicion, tides of ill will and intolerance gather darkly in many places. In our own land we enjoy indeed a fullness of life greater than that of most nations. But the rush of modern civilization itself has raised for us new difficulties, new problems which must be solved if we are to preserve to the United States the political and economic freedom for which Washington and Jefferson planned and fought.

Philadelphia is a good city in which to write American history. This is fitting ground on which to reaffirm the faith of our fathers; to pledge ourselves to restore to the people a wider freedom—to give to 1936 as the founders gave to 1776—an American way of life.

That very word freedom, in itself and of necessity, suggests freedom from some restraining power. In 1776 we sought freedom from the tyranny of a political autocracy—from the eighteenth century royalists who held special privileges from the crown. It was to perpetuate their privilege that they governed without the consent of the governed; that they denied the right of free assembly and free speech; that they restricted the worship of God; that they put the average man's property and the average man's life in pawn to the mercenaries of dynastic power—that they regimented the people.

And so it was to win freedom from the tyranny of political autocracy that the American Revolution was fought. That victory gave the business of governing into the hands of the average man, who won the right with his neighbors to make and order his own destiny through his own Government. Political tyranny was wiped out at Philadelphia on July 4, 1776.

But, since that struggle, man's inventive genius released new forces in our land which re-ordered the lives of our people. The age of machinery, of railroads, of steam and electricity; the telegraph and the radio; mass production, mass distribution—all of these combined to bring forward a new civilization and with it a problem for those who sought to remain free.

For out of this modern civilization economic royalists carved new dynasties. New Kingdoms were built upon concentration of control over material things. Through new uses of corporations, banks and securities, new machinery of industry and agriculture, of labor and capital—

all undreamed of by the fathers—the whole structure of modern life was impressed into this royal service.

There was no place among this royalty for our many thousands of small business men and merchants who sought to make a worthy use of the American system of initiative and profit. They were no more free than the worker or the farmer. Even honest and progressive-minded men of wealth, aware of their obligation to their generation, could never know just where they fitted into this dynastic scheme of things.

And so it was natural and perfectly human that the privileged princes of these new economic dynasties, thirsting for power, reached out for control over government itself. They created a new despotism and wrapped it in the robes of legal sanction. In its service new mercenaries sought to regiment the people, their labor, their property. And as a result the average man once more confronts the problem that faced the Minute Man of seventy-six.

The hours men and women worked, the wages they received, the conditions of their labor—these had passed beyond the control of the people, and were imposed by this new industrial dictatorship. The savings of the average family, the capital of the small business man, the investments set aside for old age—other people's money—these were tools which the new economic royalty used to dig itself in.

Those who tilled the soil no longer reaped the rewards which were their right. The small measure of their gains was decreed by men in distant cities.

Throughout the Nation, opportunity was limited by monopoly. Individual initiative was crushed in the cogs of a great machine. The field open for free business was more and more restricted. Private enterprise, indeed, became too private. It became privileged enterprise, not free enterprise.

An old English judge said once upon a time: "Necessitous men are not free men." Liberty requires opportunity to make a living—a living decent according to the standard of the time, a living which gives man not only enough to live by, but something to live for.

For too many of us the political equality we once had won was meaningless in the face of economic inequality. A small group had concentrated into their own hands an almost complete control over other people's property, other people's money, other people's labor—other people's lives. For too many of us life was no longer free; liberty no longer real; men could no longer follow the pursuit of happiness.

Against economic tyranny such as this, the American citizen could only appeal to the organized power of government. We will remember that the collapse of 1929 showed up the despotism for what it was. The election of 1932 was the people's mandate to end it. Under that mandate it is being ended.

The royalists I have spoken of—the royalists of the economic order have conceded that political freedom was the business of the government, but they have maintained that economic slavery was nobody's business. They granted that the government could protect the citizen in his right to vote but they denied that the goverment could do anything to protect the citizen in his right to work and his right to live.

Today we stand committed to the proposition that freedom is no half and half affair. If the average citizen is guaranteed equal opportunity in the polling place, he must have equal opportunity in the market place.

These economic royalists complain that we seek to overthrow the institutions of America. What they really complain of is that we seek to take away their power. Our allegiance to American institutions requires the overthrow of this kind of power. In vain they seek to hide behind the Flag and the Constitution. In their blindness they forget what the Flag and the Constitution stand for. Now, as always, for over a century and a half, the Flag, the Constitution, stand against a dictatorship by mob rule and the over-privileged alike, and the Flag and the Constitution stand for democracy, not tyranny; for freedom, but not subjection. . . .

It is a sobering thing, my friends, to be a servant of this great cause. We try in our daily work to remember that the cause belongs not to us but to the people. The standard is not in the hands of you and me alone. It is carried by America. We seek, all of us I hope, we seek daily to profit from experience, to learn to do better as our task proceeds.

Governments can err—Presidents do make mistakes, but the immortal Dante tells us that divine justice weighs the sins of the cold-blooded and the sins of the warm-hearted in different scales.

Better the occasional faults of a government that lives in a spirit of charity than the consistent omissions of a government frozen in the ice of its own indifference.

There is a mysterious cycle in human events. To some generations much is given. Of other generations much is expected. This generation of Americans has a rendezvous with destiny.

In this world of ours in other lands, there are some people, who, in times past, have lived and fought for freedom, and seem to have grown too weary to carry on the fight. They have sold their heritage of freedom for the illusion of a living. They have yielded their democracy.

I believe in my heart that only our success can stir their ancient hope. They begin to know that here in America we are waging a great and successful war. It is not alone a war against want and destitution and economic demoralization. It is more than that, it is a war for the

survival of democracy. We are fighting, fighting to save a great and precious form of government for ourselves and for the world.

And so I accept the commission you have tendered me. I join with
you. I am enlisted for the duration of the war.

Campaign Speech
Chicago, October 14, 1936

FDR was in fine campaigning form when he returned to Chicago on October 14, 1936 to deliver this speech with his second presidential election only a few weeks away. With the great good humor which he could always muster when the situation called for it, FDR addressed those who saw him as hostile to business. It may not have swayed many of his more implacable critics, but from all accounts his supporters greatly enjoyed it.

Mr. Chairman, Governor Horner, Mayor Kelly, my friends of the great State of Illinois:

I seem to have been here before.

Four years ago I dropped into this city from the airways—an old friend come in a new way—to accept in this hall the nomination for the Presidency of the United States. I came to a Chicago fighting with its back to the wall—factories closed, markets silent, banks shaky, ships and trains empty. Today those factories sing the song of industry—markets hum with bustling movement, banks are secure; ships and trains are running full. Once again it is a Chicago that smiles. And with Chicago a whole nation that had not been cheerful for years is full of cheer once more.

On this trip I have talked to farmers, I have talked to miners, I have talked to industrial workers—and in all that I have seen and heard one fact has been clear as crystal—that they are part and parcel of a rounded whole, and that none of them can succeed in their chosen occupations if those in the other occupations fall or fail in their prosperity. I have driven that point home.

And tonight, in this center of business of America, I give the same message to the business men of America—to those who make and sell the processed goods the Nation uses and to the men and women who work for them.

To them I say:

Do you have a deposit in the bank? It is safer today than it has ever been in our history. It is guaranteed. Last October first marked the end of the first full year in 55 years without a single failure of a national bank in the United States. Isn't that on the credit side of the government's account with you?

Are you an investor? Your stocks and bonds are up to a five and six year high level.

Are you a merchant? Your markets have the precious lifeblood of purchasing power. Your customers on the farms have better incomes and smaller debts. Your customers in the cities have more jobs, surer jobs, better jobs. Didn't your government have something to do with this?

Are you in industry? Industrial earnings, industrial profits are the highest in four, six, or even seven years! Bankruptcies are at a new low. Your government takes some credit for that.

Are you in railroads? Freight loadings are steadily going up and so are passenger receipts because, for one reason, your government made the railroads cut rates and make money.

Are you a middleman in the great stream of farm products? The meat and grain that move through your yards and elevators have a steadier supply, a steadier demand and steadier prices than you have known for years. And your government is trying to keep it that way.

Now, my friends, some people say that all this recovery has just happened. But in a complicated modern world recoveries from depressions do not just happen. The years from 1929 to 1933 when we waited for recovery just to happen, proves the point.

But in 1933, after March 4th, we did not wait—we acted. Behind the growing recovery of today is a story of deliberate government acceptance of responsibility to save business—to save the American system of private enterprise and economic democracy—a record unequalled by any modern government in history. . . .

Because we cherished our system of private property and free enterprise and were determined to preserve it as the foundation of our traditional American system, we recalled the warning of Thomas Jefferson that "widespread poverty and concentrated wealth cannot long endure side by side in a democracy."

And so our job was to preserve the American ideal of economic as well as political democracy, against the abuse of concentration of economic power that had been insidiously growing up among us in the last fifty years, particularly during the twelve years of preceding Administrations. Free economic enterprise was being weeded out at an alarming pace.

During those years of false prosperity one business after another, one small corporation after another, their resources depleted, had failed or had fallen into the lap of a bigger competitor.

A dangerous thing was happening. More than half of the corporate wealth of the country had come under the control of less than two hundred big corporations. That is not all. These huge corporations in some cases did not even try to compete with each other. They themselves were tied together by interlocking directors, interlocking bankers and interlocking lawyers.

This concentration of wealth and power has been built upon other people's money, other people's business, other people's labor. Under this concentration independent business was allowed to exist only by sufferance. It has been a menace to the social system as well as the economic system which we call American Democracy.

As a matter of practical fact, there is no excuse for it in the cold terms of industrial efficiency.

There is no excuse for it from the point of view of the average investor.

There is no excuse for it from the point of view of the independent business man.

I believe, I have always believed, and I always will believe in private enterprise as the backbone of economic well-being in the United States.

But I know, and you know, and every independent business man who has had to struggle against the competition of monopolies knows, that this concentration of economic power in all-embracing corporations does not represent private enterprise as we Americans cherish it and propose to foster it. On the contrary, it represents private enterprise which has become a kind of private government and is a power unto itself—a regimentation of other people's money and other people's lives.

Back in Kansas I spoke about bogey-men and fairy tales which the real Republican leaders, many of whom are part of this concentrated power, are using to spread fear among the American people.

You good people have heard about these fairy tales and bogey-men too. You have heard about how antagonistic to business this Administration is supposed to be. You have heard all about the dangers which the business of America is supposed to be facing if this Administration continues.

My friends, the answer to that is the record of what we have done. It was this Administration which saved the system of private profit and free enterprise after it had been dragged to the brink of ruin by these same leaders who now try to scare you.

Look at the advance in private business in the last three and a half years; and read there what we think about private business.

Today for the first time in seven years the banker, the storekeeper, the small factory owner, the industrialist, can all sit back and enjoy the company of their own ledgers. They are in the black. That is where we want them to be; that is where our policies aim that they shall be; that is where we intend them to be in the days to come.

Some of these people really forget how sick they were. But I know how sick they were. I have their fever charts. I know how the knees of all of our rugged individualists were trembling four years ago and how their hearts fluttered. They came to Washington in great numbers. Washington did not look like a dangerous bureaucracy to them then. No, it looked like an emergency hospital. And all of these distinguished patients wanted two things—a quick hypodermic to end the pain and they wanted a course of treatment to cure the disease. They wanted them in a hurry, and we gave them both. And now, my friends, most of the patients seem to be doing very nicely. Some of them are even well enough to throw their crutches at the doctor.

I believe in individualism. I believe in it in the arts, the sciences and professions. I believe in it in business. I believe in individualism in all these things—up to the point where the individualist starts to operate at the expense of society. And the overwhelming majority of American business men do not believe in it beyond that point. We have all suffered in the past from individualism run wild—society has suffered and business has suffered.

And so, believing in the solvency of business, the solvency of farmers and the solvency of workers, I believe also in the solvency of Government. Your Government is solvent.

The net Federal debt today is lower in proportion to the income of the Nation and in proportion to the wealth of the Nation than it was on March 4, 1933.

And in the future it will become lower still because with the rising tide of national income and national wealth, the very causes of our emergency spending are starting to disappear, Government expenditures are coming down and Government income is going up. And so, my friends, the opportunities for private enterprise will continue to expand.

The people of America have no quarrel with business. They insist only that the power of concentrated wealth shall not be abused.

We have come through a hard struggle to preserve democracy in America. Where other nations in other parts of the world have lost that fight, we have won it.

The businessmen of America and all other citizens have joined in a firm resolve to hold the fruits of that victory—to cling to the old ideals, to cling to the old fundamentals upon which America has grown great.

Second Inaugural Address
Washington, D.C., January 20, 1937

Some early polls had indicated that popular, moderate Al Landon might be able to make a fairly close race of the 1936 campaign since FDR and the New Deal had many opponents. As the election approached, for example, telephone operators on the switchboard of the *Chicago Tribune* had instructions to answer incoming calls by saying, "Do you know there are only —— days to save your country?" Roosevelt was unrepentant. In his last campaign appearance, at New York's Madison Square Garden on October 31st, he put it succinctly: "Never before in all our history have these forces been so united against one candidate as they stand today. They are unanimous in their hatred for me—and I welcome their hatred."

In the end, the election was a massive personal victory for FDR and the New Deal. He defeated Landon in popular votes by 27 million to 16 million, and in the electoral college by 523 to 8, winning every state but Maine and Vermont. His second inauguration, following the provisions of the twentieth amendment to the Constitution, was the first to occur on January 20th instead of the first Saturday in March. On January 20, 1937, FDR again took the oath of office on the east portico of the Capitol from Chief Justice Charles Evans Hughes. And then, in a driving rainstorm, he spoke more of the challenges yet to come—"I see one-third of a nation ill-housed, ill-clad, ill-nourished"—than what had been accomplished so far.

The American voting public had obviously endorsed the basic ideas of the New Deal, and in effect, voted for another four years of it. As they looked back on FDR's first administration, however, the electorate's collective report card must have been somewhat mixed. The banking crisis which had ushered in Roosevelt's first term had been dealt with successfully, and new regulatory legislation made a recurrence unlikely. The Civilian Conservation Corps counted as a success, employing half a million young men at its peak, and planting millions of trees and performing badly needed flood-control work. Mortgage relief had helped millions of farmers and homeowners keep their property, and the Reconstruction Finance Corporation had helped many businesses survive the darkest days. Attempts to support farm prices through subsidies for lowered production through the Agricultural Adjustment Administration were only moderately successful, however, and were made more difficult when the Supreme Court invalidated portions of the program. The drought and "dust bowl" conditions of the later years of the 1930s did more to help those farmers who survived them by effectively limiting production, but total farm income still didn't return to its 1929 level until 1941. The attempt by the National Recovery Administration to administer codes of fair practices like setting minimum wages and maximum hours was a major fiasco. The system became too complicated and was mired in ever-burgeoning complexity when the Supreme Court finally killed it in 1935. The NRA could claim some major accomplishments in collective bargaining, and regulating child labor in interstate commerce and other areas. The Social Security Act of 1935 brought the nation unemployment and old-age insurance; and the Works Progress Administration, starting in 1935, gave employment to over 2 million workers a year, and aided recovery from the Depression by channeling billions of dollars into the economy. Despite the individual programs which failed and the many setbacks it endured, the New Deal's support was solid among industrial workers, farmers, and the underprivileged in general. And the election against Landon showed that the extreme right-wing opposition to it might be vocal and intense, but couldn't in the end produce enough votes to make inroads in FDR's mandate.

When four years ago we met to inaugurate a President, the Republic, single-minded in anxiety, stood in spirit here. We dedicated ourselves to the fulfillment of a vision—to speed the time when there would be for all the people that security and peace essential to the pursuit of happiness. We of the Republic pledged ourselves to drive from the temple of our ancient faith those who had profaned it; to end by action, tireless and unafraid, the stagnation and despair of that day. We did those first things first.

Our covenant with ourselves did not stop there. Instinctively we recognized a deeper need—the need to find through government the instrument of our united purpose to solve for the individual the ever-rising problems of a complex civilization. Repeated attempts at their solution without the aid of government had left us baffled and bewildered. For, without that aid, we had been unable to create those moral controls over the services of science which are necessary to make science a useful servant instead of a ruthless master of mankind. To do this we knew that we must find practical controls over blind economic forces and blindly selfish men.

We of the Republic sensed the truth that democratic government has innate capacity to protect its people against disasters once considered inevitable, to solve problems once considered unsolvable. We would not admit that we could not find a way to master economic epidemics just as, after centuries of fatalistic suffering, we had found a way to master epidemics of disease. We refused to leave the problems of our common welfare to be solved by the winds of chance and the hurricanes of disaster.

In this we Americans were discovering no wholly new truth; we were writing a new chapter in our book of self-government.

This year marks the one hundred and fiftieth anniversary of the Constitutional Convention which made us a nation. At that Convention our forefathers found the way out of the chaos which followed the Revolutionary War; they created a strong government with powers of united action sufficient then and now to solve problems utterly beyond individual or local solution. A century and a half ago they established the Federal Government in order to promote the general welfare and secure the blessings of liberty to the American people.

Today we invoke those same powers of government to achieve the same objectives.

Four years of new experience have not belied our historic instinct. They hold out the clear hope that government within communities, government within the separate States, and government of the United States can do the things the times require, without yielding its democracy. Our tasks in the last four years did not force democracy to take a holiday.

Nearly all of us recognize that as intricacies of human relationships increase, so power to govern them also must increase—power to stop evil; power to do good. The essential democracy of our Nation and the safety of our people depend not upon the absence of power, but upon lodging it with those whom the people can change or continue at stated intervals through an honest and free system of elections. The Constitution of 1787 did not make our democracy impotent.

In fact, in these last four years, we have made the exercise of all power more democratic; for we have begun to bring private autocratic powers into their proper subordination to the public's government. The legend that they were invincible—above and beyond the processes of a democracy—has been shattered. They have been challenged and beaten.

Our progress out of the depression is obvious. But that is not all that you and I mean by the new order of things. Our pledge was not merely to do a patchwork job with secondhand materials. By using the new materials of social justice we have undertaken to erect on the old foundations a more enduring structure for the better use of future generations.

In that purpose we have been helped by achievements of mind and spirit. Old truths have been relearned; untruths have been unlearned. We have always known that heedless self-interest was bad morals; we know now that it is bad economics. Out of the collapse of a prosperity whose builders boasted their practicality has come the conviction that in the long run economic morality pays. We are beginning to wipe out the line that divides the practical from the ideal; and in so doing we are fashioning an instrument of unimagined power for the establishment of a morally better world.

This new understanding undermines the old admiration of wordly success as such. We are beginning to abandon our tolerance of the abuse of power by those who betray for profit the elementary decencies of life.

In this process evil things formerly accepted will not be so easily condoned. Hard-headedness will not so easily excuse hardheartedness. We are moving toward an era of good feeling. But we realize that there can be no era of good feeling save among men of good will.

For these reasons I am justified in believing that the greatest change we have witnessed has been the change in the moral climate of America.

Among men of good will, science and democracy together offer an ever-richer life and ever-larger satisfaction to the individual. With this change in our moral climate and our rediscovered ability to improve our economic order, we have set our feet upon the road of enduring progress.

Shall we pause now and turn our back upon the road that lies ahead? Shall we call this the promised land? Or, shall we continue on our way? For "each age is a dream that is dying, or one that is coming to birth."

Many voices are heard as we face a great decision. Comfort says, "Tarry a while." Opportunism says, "This is a good spot." Timidity asks, "How difficult is the road ahead?"

True, we have come far from the days of stagnation and despair. Vitality has been preserved. Courage and confidence have been restored. Mental and moral horizons have been extended.

But our present gains were won under the pressure of more than ordinary circumstances. Advance became imperative under the goad of fear and suffering. The times were on the side of progress.

To hold to progress today, however, is more difficult. Dulled conscience, irresponsibility, and ruthless self-interest already reappear. Such symptoms of prosperity may become portents of disaster! Prosperity already tests the persistence of our progressive purpose.

Let us ask again: Have we reached the goal of our vision of that fourth day of March 1933? Have we found our happy valley?

I see a great nation, upon a great continent, blessed with a great wealth of natural resources. Its hundred and thirty million people are at peace among themselves; they are making their country a good neighbor among the nations. I see a United States which can demonstrate that, under democratic methods of government, national wealth can be translated into a spreading volume of human comforts hitherto unknown, and the lowest standard of living can be raised far above the level of mere subsistence.

But here is the challenge to our democracy: In this nation I see tens of millions of its citizens—a substantial part of its whole population—who at this very moment are denied the greater part of what the very lowest standards of today call the necessities of life.

I see millions of families trying to live on incomes so meager that the pall of family disaster hangs over them day by day.

I see millions whose daily lives in city and on farm continue under conditions labeled indecent by a so-called polite society half a century ago.

I see millions denied education, recreation, and the opportunity to better their lot and the lot of their children.

I see millions lacking the means to buy the products of farm and factory and by their poverty denying work and productiveness to many other millions.

I see one-third of a nation ill-housed, ill-clad, ill-nourished.

It is not in despair that I paint you that picture. I paint it for you in hope—because the Nation, seeing and understanding the injustice in it, proposes to paint it out. We are determined to make every American citizen the subject of his country's interest and concern; and we will never regard any faithful law-abiding group within our borders as superfluous. The test of our progress is not whether we add more to the abundance of those who have much; it is whether we provide enough for those who have too little.

If I know aught of the spirit and purpose of our Nation, we will not listen to Comfort, Opportunism, and Timidity. We will carry on.

Overwhelmingly, we of the Republic are men and women of good will; men and women who have more than warm hearts of dedication; men and women who have cool heads and willing hands of practical purpose as well. They will insist that every agency of popular government use effective instruments to carry out their will.

Government is competent when all who compose it work as trustees for the whole people. It can make constant progress when it keeps abreast of all the facts. It can obtain justified support and legitimate criticism when the people receive true information of all that government does.

If I know aught of the will of our people, they will demand that these conditions of effective government shall be created and maintained. They will demand a nation uncorrupted by cancers of injustice and, therefore, strong among the nations in its example of the will to peace.

Today we reconsecrate our country to long-cherished ideals in a suddenly changed civilization. In every land there are always at work forces that drive men apart and forces that draw men together. In our personal ambitions we are individualists. But in our seeking for economic and political progress as a nation, we all go up, or else we all go down, as one people.

To maintain a democracy of effort requires a vast amount of patience in dealing with differing methods, a vast amount of humility. But out of the confusion of many voices rises an understanding of dominant public need. Then political leadership can voice common ideals, and aid in their realization.

In taking again the oath of office as President of the United States, I assume the solemn obligation of leading the American people forward along the road over which they have chosen to advance.

While this duty rests upon me I shall do my utmost to speak their purpose and to do their will, seeking Divine guidance to help us each and every one to give light to them that sit in darkness and to guide our feet into the way of peace.

Quarantine Address
Chicago, October 5, 1937

International tensions escalated steadily throughout the middle years of the 1930s. 1935 saw Mussolini's invasion of Abyssinia; 1936, the Spanish Civil War and the success of the fascists against the Spanish Republic. It was Japanese military action in northern China in 1937, however, which provided the immediate context for this major foreign policy address which FDR gave in Chicago on October 5th. Beginning a major push in July, within a few months Japanese forces had overrun Peking and were threatening Nanking. American newsreel audiences had been horrified by graphic pictures of Japanese bombs falling on helpless Chinese civilians; and in China, the American ambassador and his staff had been forced to retreat from their embassy to American gunboats stationed in the Yangtze River. In FDR's thinking, Japan had clearly joined Germany and Italy as one of the group of nations most responsible for the world's instability. So when he gave this speech in the heart of the isolationist Midwest, FDR was testing the domestic political waters for support for a stronger national policy against unchecked aggression than could be provided under the Neutrality Act then on the books.

The thesis of the speech was simple. Aggression was like a contagious fever, and non-aggressive nations should "quarantine" the lawless and aggressive ones, and isolate them from the rest of the world. On how this would play out in the realm of practical action, however, FDR was no doubt intentionally vague. He knew there would be little support at home for a policy which would bring America into armed conflict with the perpetrator of any aggressive act; and to most astute observers, he seemed to be suggesting the cessation of diplomatic relations with aggressors, and cutting off trade with them—thereby keeping them from acquiring basic raw materials. Japan, with its total reliance on foreign trade for oil, was a perfect case in point. The speech created a brief but major news sensation, and for a day or two challenged the

World Series for the featured spot in the nation's headlines. The overall political reaction was generally favorable, although the most ardent isolationists raised the specter of the United States being dragged into foreign wars by politicians in general, and Roosevelt in particular. In the end, however, perhaps because of its vagueness in terms of actual policy steps, the quarantine idea failed to produce any real result. Japan continued to ransack China, and Europe continued to slide down the slope toward all-out war.

Mayor Kelly, Governor Horner, my friends in Chicago:

. . . It is because the people of the United States must, for the sake of their own future, give thought to the rest of the world, that I, as the responsible executive head of the Nation, have chosen this great inland city and this gala occasion to speak to you on a subject of definite national importance.

The political situation in the world, which of late has been growing progressively worse, is such as to cause grave concern and anxiety to all the peoples and nations who wish to live in peace and amity with their neighbors.

Some fifteen years ago the hopes of mankind for a continuing era of international peace were raised to great heights when more than sixty nations solemnly pledged themselves not to resort to arms in furtherance of their national aims and policies. The high aspirations expressed in the Briand-Kellogg Peace Pact and the hopes for peace thus raised have of late given way to a haunting fear of calamity. The present reign of terror and international lawlessness began a few years ago.

It began through unjustified interference in the internal affairs of other nations or the invasion of alien territory in violation of treaties. It has now reached a stage where the very foundations of civilization are seriously threatened. The landmarks, the traditions which have marked the progress of civilization toward a condition of law and order and justice are being wiped away.

Without a declaration of war and without warning or justification of any kind civilians, including vast numbers of women and children, are being ruthlessly murdered with bombs from the air. In times of so-called peace ships are being attacked and sunk by submarines without cause or notice. Nations are fomenting and taking sides in civil warfare in nations that have never done them any harm. Nations claiming freedom for themselves deny it to others.

Innocent peoples, innocent nations are being cruelly sacrificed to a greed for power and supremacy which is devoid of all sense of justice and humane consideration.

To paraphrase a recent author "perhaps we foresee a time when men, exultant in the technique of homicide, will rage so hotly over the world that every precious thing will be in danger, every book, every picture, every harmony, every treasure garnered through two milleniums, the small, the delicate, the defenseless—all will be lost or wrecked or utterly destroyed."

If those things come to pass in other parts of the world, let no one imagine that America will escape, that America may expect mercy, that this Western Hemisphere will not be attacked and that it will continue tranquilly and peacefully to carry on the ethics and the arts of civilization.

No, if those days come "there will be no safety by arms, no help from authority, no answer in science. The storm will rage till every flower of culture is trampled and all human beings are leveled in a vast chaos."

If those days are not to come to pass—if we are to have a world in which we can breathe freely and live in amity without fear—then the peace-loving nations must make a concerted effort to uphold laws and principles on which alone peace can rest secure.

The peace-loving nations must make a concerted effort in opposition to those violations of treaties and those ignorings of humane instincts which today are creating a state of international anarchy, international instability from which there is no escape through mere isolation or neutrality.

Those who cherish their freedom and recognize and respect the equal rights of their neighbors to be free and live in peace, must work together for the triumph of law and moral principles in order that peace, justice and confidence may prevail throughout the world. There must be a return to a belief in the pledged word, in the value of a signed treaty. There must be recognition of the fact that national morality is as vital as private morality.

A bishop wrote to me the other day: "It seems to me that something greatly needs to be said in behalf of ordinary humanity against the present practice of carrying the horrors of war to helpless civilians, especially women and children. It may be that such a protest may be regarded by many, who claim to be realists, as futile, but may it not be that the heart of mankind is so filled with horror at the present needless suffering that that force could be mobilized in sufficient volume to lessen such cruelty in the days ahead. Even though it may take twenty years, which God forbid, for civilization to make effective its corporate protest against this barbarism, surely strong voices may hasten the day."

There is a solidarity, an interdependence about the modern world, both technically and morally, which makes it impossible for any nation completely to isolate itself from political and economic upheavals in the rest of the world, especially when such upheavals appear to be spreading and not declining. There can be no stability or peace either within nations or between nations except under laws and moral standards adhered to by all. International anarchy destroys every foundation for peace. It jeopardizes either the immediate or the future security of every nation, large or small. And it is, therefore, a matter of vital interest and concern to the people of the United States that the sanctity of international treaties and the maintenance of international morality be restored.

The overwhelming majority of all the peoples and nations of the world today want to live in peace. They seek the removal of barriers against trade. They want to exert themselves in industry, in agriculture, in business, that they may increase their wealth through the production of wealth-producing goods rather than striving to produce military planes and bombs and machine guns and cannon for the destruction of human lives and useful property.

In those nations of the world which seem to be piling armament on armament for purposes of aggression, and those other nations which fear acts of aggression against them and their security, a very high proportion of their national income is being spent directly for armaments. It runs from thirty to as high as fifty per cent in most of those cases.

We are fortunate. The proportion that we spend in the United States is far less—eleven or twelve per cent.

How happy we are that the circumstances of the moment permit us to put our money into bridges and boulevards, dams and reforestation, the conservation of our soil and many other kinds of useful works rather than into huge standing armies and vast supplies of implements of war.

Nevertheless, my friends, I am compelled and you are compelled to look ahead. The peace, the freedom, the security of ninety per cent of the population of the world is being jeopardized by the remaining ten per cent who are threatening a breakdown of all international order and law. Surely the ninety per cent who want to live in peace under law and in accordance with moral standards that have received almost universal acceptance through the centuries, can and must find some way to make their will prevail.

Yes, the situation is definitely of universal concern. The questions involved relate not merely to violations of specific provisions of particular treaties; they are questions of war and peace, of international law and especially of principles of humanity. It is true that they involve definite violations of agreements, and especially of the Covenant of the League of Nations, the Briand-Kellogg Pact and the Nine Power Treaty. And we have signed both of the last two. But they involve also problems of world economy, world security and world humanity.

It is true that the moral consciousness of the world must recognize the importance of removing injustices and well-founded grievances; but at the same time it must be aroused to the cardinal necessity of honoring sanctity of treaties, of respecting the rights and liberties of others and of putting an end to acts of international aggression.

It seems to be unfortunately true that the epidemic of world lawlessness is spreading.

And mark this well! When an epidemic of physical disease starts to spread, the community approves and joins in a quarantine of the patients in order to protect the health of the community against the spread of the disease.

It is my determination to pursue a policy of peace. It is my determination to adopt every practicable measure to avoid involvement in war. It ought to be inconceivable that in this modern era, and in the face of experience, any nation could be so foolish and ruthless as to run the risk of plunging the whole world into war by invading and violating in contravention of solemn treaties, the territory of other nations that have done them no real harm and which are too weak to protect themselves adequately. Yet the peace of the world and the welfare and security of every nation, including our own, is today being threatened by that very thing.

No nation which refuses to exercise forbearance and to respect the freedom and rights of others can long remain strong and retain the confidence and respect of other nations. No nation ever loses its dignity or its good standing by conciliating its differences, and by exercising great patience, patience with, and consideration for, the rights of other nations.

War is a contagion, whether it be declared or undeclared. It can engulf states and peoples remote from the original scene of hostilities. Yes, we are determined to keep out of war, yet we cannot insure ourselves against the disastrous effects of war and the dangers of involvement. We are adopting such measures as will minimize our risk of involvement but we cannot have complete protection in a world of disorder in which confidence and security have broken down.

If civilization is to survive the principles of the Prince of Peace must be restored. Shattered trust between nations must be revived.

Most important of all, the will for peace on the part of peace-loving nations must express itself to the end that nations that may be tempted to violate their agreements and the rights of others will desist from such a cause. There must be positive endeavors to preserve peace.

America hates war. America hopes for peace. Therefore, America actively engages in the search for peace.

Fireside Chat (on the Outbreak of World War II)

Washington, D.C., September 3, 1939

FDR first learned of the onset of World War II when he received a telephone call from the American ambassador in Paris, William C. Bullitt, at 2:50 A.M. on September 1, 1939. Bullitt was relaying news from Warsaw that German troops had invaded Poland. Later that morning, Joseph P. Kennedy, America's ambassador in England, called to say that the British Prime Minister Neville Chamberlain had informed him that Britain would also go to war over the German invasion of Poland. The British and French officially declared war on Germany on September 3rd, and on that day, Roosevelt broadcast his Fireside Chat to the American public. In it he outlined the country's position as officially neutral as was required of him by the Neutrality Act. "This nation will remain a neutral nation," he began, "but I cannot ask that every American remain neutral in thought as well."

My Fellow Americans and My Friends:

Tonight my single duty is to speak to the whole of America.

Until four-thirty this morning I had hoped against hope that some miracle would prevent a devastating war in Europe and bring to an end the invasion of Poland by Germany.

For four long years a succession of actual wars and constant crises have shaken the entire world and have threatened in each case to bring on the gigantic conflict which is today unhappily a fact.

It is right that I should recall to your minds the consistent and at time successful efforts of your Government in these crises to throw the full weight of the United States into the cause of peace. In spite of spreading wars I think that we have every right and every reason to maintain as a national policy the fundamental moralities, the teachings of religion [and] the continuation of efforts to restore peace—because some day, though the time may be distant, we can be of even greater help to a crippled humanity.

It is right, too, to point out that the unfortunate events of these recent years have, without question, been based on the use of force and the threat of force. And it seems to me clear, even at the outbreak of this great war, that the influence of America should be consistent in seeking for humanity a final peace which will eliminate, as far as it is possible to do so, the continued use of force between nations.

It is, of course, impossible to predict the future. I have my constant stream of information from American representatives and other sources throughout the world. You, the people of this country, are receiving news through your radios and your newspapers at every hour of the day.

You are, I believe, the most enlightened and the best informed people in all the world at this moment. You are subjected to no censorship of news, and I want to add that your Government has no information which it withholds [from you] or which it has any thought of withholding from you.

At the same time, as I told my Press Conference on Friday, it is of the highest importance that the press and the radio use the utmost caution to discriminate between actual verified fact on the one hand, and mere rumor on the other.

I can add to that by saying that I hope the people of this country will also discriminate most carefully between news and rumor. Do not believe of necessity everything you hear or read. Check up on it first.

You must master at the outset a simple but unalterable fact in modern foreign relations between nations. When peace has been broken anywhere, the peace of all countries everywhere is in danger.

It is easy for you and for me to shrug our shoulders and to say that conflicts taking place thousands of miles from the continental United States, and, indeed, thousands of miles from the whole American Hemisphere, do not seriously affect the Americas—and that all the United States has to do is to ignore them and go about its own business. Passionately though we may desire detachment, we are forced to realize that every word that comes through the air, every ship that sails the sea, every battle that is fought does affect the American future.

Let no man or woman thoughtlessly or falsely talk of America sending its armies to European fields. At this moment there is being prepared a proclamation of American neutrality. This would have been done even if there had been no neutrality statute on the books, for this proclamation is in accordance with international law and in accordance with American policy.

This will be followed by a Proclamation required by the existing Neutrality Act. And I trust that in the days to come our neutrality can be made a true neutrality.

It is of the utmost importance that the people of this country, with the best information in the world, think things through. The most dangerous enemies of American peace are those who, without well-rounded Information on the whole broad subject of the past, the present and the future, undertake to speak with assumed authority, to talk in terms of glittering generalities, to give to the nation assurances or prophecies which are of little present or future value.

I myself cannot and do not prophesy the course of events abroad—and the reason is that because I have of necessity such a complete picture of what is going on in every part of the world, that I do not dare to do so. And the other reason is that I think it is honest for me to be honest with the people of the United States.

I cannot prophesy the immediate economic effect of this new war on our nation but I do say that no American has the moral right to profiteer at the expense either of his fellow citizens or of the men, the women and the children who are living and dying in the midst of war in Europe.

Some things we do know. Most of us in the United States believe in spiritual values. Most of us, regardless of what church we belong to, believe in the spirit of the New Testament—a great teaching which opposes itself to the use of force, of armed force, of marching armies and falling bombs. The overwhelming masses of our people seek peace—peace at home, and the kind of peace in other lands which will not jeopardize our peace at home.

We have certain ideas and certain ideals of national safety and we must act to preserve that safety today and to preserve the safety of our children in future years.

That safety is and will be bound up with the safety of the Western Hemisphere and of the seas adjacent thereto. We seek to keep war from our own firesides by keeping war from coming to the Americas. For that we have historic precedent that goes back to the days of the Administration of President George Washington. It is serious enough and tragic enough to every American family in every state in the Union to live in a world that is torn by wars on other Continents. And those wars today affect every American home. It is our national duty to use every effort to keep those wars out of the Americas.

And at this time let me make the simple plea that partisanship and selfishness be adjourned; and that national unity be the thought that underlies all others.

This nation will remain a neutral nation, but I cannot ask that every American remain neutral in thought as well. Even a neutral has a right to take account of facts. Even a neutral cannot be asked to close his mind or close his conscience.

I have said not once but many times that I have seen war and that I hate war. I say that again and again.

I hope the United States will keep out of this war. I believe that it will. And I give you assurance[s] and reassurance that every effort of your Government will be directed toward that end.

As long as it remains within my power to prevent, there will be no blackout of peace in the United States.

"Dagger in the Back"
Charlottesville, June 10, 1940

Reacting with contempt to news of Mussolini's declaration of war against France—a nation already on the brink of military collapse—Roosevelt added his memorable "dagger in the back" reference to the prepared text of a commencement address he gave on June 10, 1940 at the University of Virginia where his son, Franklin, Jr., was among the law school graduates: "On this tenth day of June, 1940, the hand that held the dagger has struck it into the back of its neighbor." Sumner Welles, FDR's under secretary of state, had urged Roosevelt not to use this provocative phrase, and thought he had won the argument; but at the last moment, FDR reinserted it and came away feeling vindicated by the warm reception his remarks received from the Virginia students and faculty. The overall political response from around the country was also favorable.

The theme which Roosevelt underscored in this and all of his speeches on foreign policy leading up to World War II, was the necessity of aiding Great Britain and other democracies in their struggle against Nazi Germany. The Neutrality Act prevented the United States from simply giving war materials to anyone, and as an officially neutral nation, we were precluded by the Hague Convention from supplying arms directly to any belligerent nation. Ways had to be found to supply those arms indirectly, generally through the agency of private corporations; but the furor raised by isolationist elements whenever increased military aid was broached made it immensely difficult for Roosevelt to find ways to provide Britain with the level of aid which he knew was needed. The fall of France in 1940 brought FDR new support at home for increased aid to Great Britain, and the passage of Lend-Lease the following year made it easier to provide that aid; but this great national argument really ended only with Pearl Harbor.

President Newcomb, my friends of the University of Virginia:

I notice by the program that I am asked to address the classes of 1940. I avail myself of that privilege, but I also take this very happy occasion to speak to many other classes—classes that have graduated through all the years, classes that are still in the period of study, classes not alone of the schools of learning of the nation, but classes that have come up through the great schools of experience. In other words, a cross-section, a cross-section just as you who graduate today are a cross-section of the nation as a whole.

Every generation of young men and women in America has questions to ask the world. Most of the time they are the simple but nevertheless difficult questions—questions of work to do, opportunities to find, ambitions to satisfy.

But every now and again in the history of the republic a different kind of question presents itself—a question that asks, not about the future of an individual or even of a generation, but about the future of the country, the future of the American people.

There was such a time at the beginning of our history, at the beginning of our history as a nation. Young people asked themselves in those days what lay ahead, not for themselves, but for the new United States.

There was such a time again in the seemingly endless years of the war between the States. Young men and young women on both sides of the line asked themselves, not what trades or professions they would enter, what lives they would make, but what was to become of the country they had known.

There is such a time again today. Again today the young men and the young women of America ask themselves with earnestness and with deep concern this same question: "What is to become of the country we know?"

Now they ask it with even greater anxiety than before. They ask, not only what the future holds for this republic, but what the future holds for all peoples and all nations that have been living under democratic forms of government—under the free institutions of a free people.

It is understandable to all of us, I think, that they should ask this question. They read the words of those who are telling them that the ideal of individual liberty, the ideal of free franchise, the ideal of peace through justice is a decadent ideal.

They read the word and hear the boast of those who say that a belief in force—force directed by self-chosen leaders—is the new and vigorous system which will overrun the earth. They have seen the ascendency of this philosophy of force in nation after nation where free institutions and individual liberties were once maintained.

It is natural and understandable that the younger generation should first ask itself what the extension of the philosophy of force to all the world would lead to ultimately. We see today, for example, in stark reality some of the consequences of what we call the machine age.

Where control of machines has been retained in the hands of mankind as a whole, untotaled benefits have accrued to mankind. For mankind was then the master: The machine was the servant.

But in this new system of force the mastery of the machine is not in the hands of mankind. It is in the control of infinitely small groups of individuals who rule without a single one of the democratic sanctions that we have known.

The machine in the hands of irresponsible conquerors becomes the master; mankind is not only the servant, it is the victim too. Such mastery abandons with deliberate contempt all of the moral values to which even this young country for more than 300 years has been accustomed and dedicated.

Surely the new philosophy proves from month to month that it could have no possible conception of the way of life or the way of thought of a nation whose origins go back to Jamestown and Plymouth Rock.

And conversely, neither those who spring from that ancient stock nor those who have come hither in later years can be indifferent to the destruction of freedom in their ancestral lands across the sea.

Perception of danger to our institutions may come slowly or it may come with a rush and shock as it has to the people of the United States in the past few months. This perception of danger—danger in a world-wide arena—has come to us clearly and overwhelmingly. We perceive the peril in this world-wide arena—an arena that may become so narrow that only the Americas will retain the ancient faiths.

Some indeed still hold to the now somewhat obvious delusion that we of the United States can safely permit the United States to become a lone island, a lone island in a world dominated by the philosophy of force.

Such an island may be the dream of those who still talk and vote as isolationists. Such an island represents to me and to the overwhelming majority of Americans today a helpless nightmare, the helpless nightmare of a people without freedom. Yes, the nightmare of a people lodged in prison, handcuffed, hungry and fed through the bars from day to day by the contemptuous, unpitying masters of other continents.

It is natural also that we should ask ourselves how now we can prevent the building of that prison and the placing of ourselves in the midst of it.

Let us not hesitate—all of us—to proclaim certain truths. Overwhelmingly we, as a nation, and this applies to all the other American nations, we are convinced that military and naval victory for the gods of force and hate would endanger the institutions of democracy in the Western World—and that equally, therefore, the whole of our sympathies lie with those nations that are giving their life blood in combat against those forces.

The people and Government of the United States have seen with the utmost regret and with grave disquiet the decision of the Italian Government to engage in the hostilities now raging in Europe.

More than three months ago the chief of the Italian Government sent me word that because of the determination of Italy to limit, so far as might be possible, the spread of the European conflict, more than two hundred millions of people in the region of the Mediterranean had been enabled to escape the suffering and the devastation of war.

I informed the chief of the Italian Government that this desire on the part of Italy to prevent the war from spreading met with full sympathy and response on the part of the government and the people of the United States, and I expressed the earnest hope of this government and of this people that this policy on the part of Italy might be continued. I made it clear that in the opinion of the Government of the United States any extension of hostilities in the region of the Mediterranean might result in the still greater enlargement of the scene of the conflict, the conflict in the Near East and in Africa, and that if this came to pass no one could foretell how much greater the theatre of war eventually might become.

Again, upon a subsequent occasion, not so far ago, recognizing that certain aspirations of Italy might form the basis of discussions between the powers most specifically concerned, I offered, in a message addressed to the chief of the Italian Government, to send to the Governments of France and Great Britain such specific indications of the desires of Italy to obtain readjustments with regard to her position as the chief of the Italian Government might desire to transmit through me.

While making it clear that the government of the United States in such an event could not and would not assume responsibility for the nature of the proposals submitted nor for agreements which might thereafter be reached, I proposed that if Italy would refrain from entering the war I would be willing to ask assurances from the other powers concerned that they would faithfully execute any agreement so reached, and that Italy's voice in any future peace conference would have the same authority as if Italy had actually taken part in the war as a belligerent.

Unfortunately, unfortunately to the regret of all of us, and to the regret of humanity, the chief of the Italian Government was unwilling to accept the procedure suggested, and he has made no counter-proposal.

This government directed its efforts to doing what it could to work for the preservation of peace in the Mediterranean area, and it likewise expressed its willingness to endeavor to cooperate with the government of Italy when the appropriate occasion arose for the creation of a more stable world order, through the reduction of armaments and through the construction of a more liberal international economic system which would assure to all powers equality of opportunity in the world markets and in the securing of raw materials on equal terms.

I have likewise, of course, felt it necessary in my communications to Signor Mussolini to express the concern of the government of the United States because of the fact that any extension of the war in the region of the Mediterranean would inevitably result in great prejudice to the ways of life and government and to the trade and commerce of all the American republics.

The government of Italy has now chosen to preserve what it terms its "freedom of action" and to fulfill what it states are its promises to Germany. In so doing it has manifested disregard for the rights and security of other nations, disregard for the lives of the peoples of those nations which are directly threatened by the spread of this war; and has evinced its unwillingness to find the means through Pacific negotiations for the satisfaction of what it believes are its legitimate aspirations.

On this 10th day of June, 1940, the hand that held the dagger has struck it into the back of its neighbor.

On this 10th day of June, 1940, in this university founded by the first great American teacher of democracy, we send forth our prayers and our hopes to those beyond the seas who are maintaining with magnificent valor their battle for freedom.

In our unity, in our American unity, we will pursue two obvious and simultaneous courses; we will extend to the opponents of force the material resources of this nation and, at the same time, we will harness and speed up the use of those resources in order that we ourselves in the Americas may have equipment and training equal to the task of any emergency and every defense.

All roads leading to the accomplishment of these objectives must be kept clear of obstructions. We will not slow down or detour. Signs and signals call for speed—full speed ahead.

Yes, it is right that each new generation should ask questions. But in recent months the principal question has been somewhat simplified. Once more the future of the nation and the future of the American people is at stake.

We need not and we will not, in any way, abandon our continuing efforts to make democracy work within our borders. Yes, we still insist on the need for vast improvements in our own social and economic life.

But that, that is a component part of national defense itself.

The program unfolds swiftly and into that program will fit the responsibility and the opportunity of every man and woman in the land to preserve our heritage in days of peril.

I call for effort, courage, sacrifice, devotion. Granting the love of freedom, all of these are possible.

And the love of freedom is still fierce, still steady in the nation today.

Press Conference

Washington, D.C., December 17, 1940

Following his victory over Wendell Wilkie in the 1940 presidential election, FDR returned from a post-election Caribbean cruise with plans for an unprecedented third term; and, above all, with a new fully-hatched scheme for providing Great Britain with the tools of war on a vastly expanded basis—the program which would eventually be called Lend-Lease. At a White House press conference on December 17, 1940, he gave his famous exposition of the Lend-Lease plan, using the analogy of a man with a hose whose neighbor's house is on fire. The idea behind Lend-Lease—that we would give Britain the materiel they needed now, and it would be paid for "in kind or property, or any other direct or indirect benefit" when the war was over—was a fiction. And Roosevelt knew it was a fiction when he expounded it. Lend-Lease represented the solution he needed both to neutralize the objections of isolationists and make the program palatable to Congress; it was enacted into law in March, 1941. At first directed to Great Britain, eventually China, Russia and many other nations received aid under Lend-Lease. Overall, the law gave the president the power to provide assistance to any nation whose defense he deemed vital to the United States in return for payment in virtually any form he found satisfactory. Most of the more than $49 billion so expended was, of course, never repaid in any form; but by the end of World War II, the issue had faded in significance.

. . . I don't think there is any particular news, except possibly one thing that I think is worth my talking about from—what will I call it?—the background method. In the present world situation of course there is absolutely no doubt in the mind of a very overwhelming number of Americans that the best immediate defense of the United States is the success of Great Britain in defending itself, and that, therefore, quite aside from our historic and current interest in the survival of democracy as a whole in the world, it is equally important from a self-ish point of view of American defense that we should do everything to help the British Empire to defend itself.

I have read a great deal of nonsense by people who can only think in what we may call traditional terms, in the last few days, about finances. Steve (Mr. Early) was asking me about it this morning, and I thought it was better that I should talk to you than for Steve to talk to you; but I gave him one line which he would have used this morning if anybody had asked him, and that was this: In my memory and your memory and in all history no major war has ever been won or lost through a lack of money. . . .

I go back to the idea that one thing that is necessary for American national defense is additional productive facilities; and the more we increase those facilities—factories, shipbuilding ways, munition plants, et cetera and so on—the stronger American national defense is. Now, orders from Great Britain are therefore a tremendous asset to American national defense, because they create, automatically, additional facilities. I am talking selfishly, from the American point of view—nothing else. Therefore, from the selfish point of view, that production must be encouraged by us; and there are several ways of encouraging it—not just one, the way the narrow-minded fellow I have been talking about might assume, and has assumed. He has assumed that the only way was to repeal certain existing statutes, like the Neutrality Act and the old Johnson Act and a few other things like that, and then lend the money to Great Britain to be spent over here—either lend it through, as was done in the earlier days of the previous war, private banking circles or make it a loan from this Government to another government—the British Government.

Well, that is the—what will I call it? the banal (you will have to find another word for banal) the banal type of mind that can only think of that method.

There is another one which is also somewhat banal—we may come to it, I don't know—and that is a gift; in other words, for us to pay for all these munitions, ships, plants, guns, et cetera, and make a gift of them to Great Britain. I am not at all sure that that is a necessity, and I am not at all sure that Great Britain would care to have a gift from the United States—the taxpayers of the United States. I doubt it very much.

Well, there are other ways, and those ways are being explored; but they are possible. All I can do is to speak in very general terms, because we are in the middle of it. I have been at it now three or four weeks, exploring other methods of continuing the building up of our productive facilities and continuing the flow of munitions to Great Britain automatically; and I will just put it this way, as not a final other method but as one of possibly several other methods that might be devised toward that end. It is possible—I will put it that way—for the United States to take over British orders, and, because they are essentially the same kind of munitions that we use ourselves, turn them into American orders. We have got enough money to do it. And thereupon such portion of them as the military events of the future would determine to be right and proper for us to allow to go to the other side, either lease the materials or sell the materials subject to mortgage to the people on the other side, on the general theory that it may still prove true that the best defense of Great Britain is the best defense of the United States, and therefore that they would be more useful to the defense of the United States if they were used in Great Britain than if they were kept in storage here.

Now, what I am trying to do is to eliminate the dollar sign, and that is something brand new in the thoughts of practically everybody in this room, I think—get rid of the silly, foolish old dollar sign. All right!

Well, let me give you an illustration: Suppose my neighbor's home catches fire, and I have got a length of garden hose four or five hundred feet away; but, by Heaven, if he can take my garden hose and connect it up with his hydrant, I may help him to put out his fire. Now, what do I do? I don't say to him before that operation, "Neighbor, my garden hose cost me $15; you have got to pay me $15 for it." What is the transaction that goes on? I don't want $15—I want my garden hose back after the fire is over. All right. If it goes through the fire all right, intact, without any damage to it, he gives it back to me and thanks me very much for the use of it. But suppose it gets smashed up—holes in it— during the fire; we don't have to have too much formality about it, but I say to him, "I was glad to lend you that hose; I see I can't use it any more, it's all smashed up." He says, "How many feet of it were there?" I tell him, "There were 150 feet of it." He says, "All right, I will replace it." Now, if I get a nice garden hose back, I am in pretty good shape. In others words, if you lend certain munitions and get the munitions back at the end of the war, if they are intact—haven't been hurt—you are all right; if they have been damaged or deteriorated or lost completely, it seems to me you come out pretty well if you have them replaced by the fellow that you have lent them to.

I can't go into details, and there is no use asking legal questions about how you would do it, because that is the thing that is now under study; but the thought—the bright thought—is that we would take over not all but a very large number of future British orders, and when they come off the line, whether they were planes or guns or something else, we would enter into some kind of arrangement for their use by the

British on the ground that it was the best thing for American defense, and that when the show was over we would get repaid in kind sometime, thereby leaving out the dollar mark in the form of a dollar debt and substituting for it a gentleman's obligation to repay in kind. I think you all get it. . . .

Fireside Chat ("The Arsenal of Democracy")
Washington, D.C., December 29, 1940

Two weeks after the press conference at which he had broached the idea of Lend-Lease, FDR went to the people in a Fireside Chat—by now he was using the phrase himself to describe these talks—on the urgency of aid to the nations at war with the Axis powers. Referring to the treaty which had formalized the creation of the Axis on September 27, 1940, Roosevelt characterized the American situation in plain terms: "Never before since Jamestown and Plymouth Rock has our American civilization been in such danger as now." To those who felt fascism could be appeased, he pointed to the recent history of Austria, Czechoslovakia, Poland, Norway, Belgium, the Netherlands, Denmark, and France. For those who hoped to keep America out of the war, he argued, our first line of defense were the nations already at war who needed our help with ships, planes, guns, and tanks. Defining his program, he once again borrowed a phrase others had used and made it his own: "We must be the great arsenal of democracy."

My Friends:

This is not a fireside chat on war. It is a talk on national security; because the nub of the whole purpose of your President is to keep you now, and your children later, and your grandchildren much later, out of a last-ditch war for the preservation of American independence and all of the things that American independence means to you and to me and to ours.

Tonight, in the presence of a world crisis, my mind goes back eight years to a night in the midst of a domestic crisis. It was a time when the wheels of American industry were grinding to a full stop, when the whole banking system of our country had ceased to function.

I well remember that while I sat in my study in the White House, preparing to talk with the people of the United States, I had before my eyes the picture of all those Americans with whom I was talking. I saw the workmen in the mills, the mines, the factories; the girl behind the counter; the small shopkeeper; the farmer doing his Spring plowing; the widows and the old men wondering about their life's savings.

I tried to convey to the great mass of American people what the banking crisis meant to them in their daily lives.

Tonight I want to do the same thing, with the same people, in this new crisis which faces America.

We met the issue in 1933 with courage and realism. We face this new crisis—this new threat to the security of our nation—with the same courage and realism.

Never before since Jamestown and Plymouth Rock has our American civilization been in such danger as now.

For on September 27, 1940—this year—by an agreement signed in Berlin, three powerful nations, two in Europe and one in Asia, joined themselves together in the threat that if the United States of America interferred with or blocked the expansion program of these three nations—a program aimed at world control—they would unite in ultimate action against the United States.

The Nazi masters of Germany have made it clear that they intend not only to dominate all life and thought in their own country, but also to enslave the whole of Europe, and then to use the resources of Europe to dominate the rest of the world.

It was only three weeks ago that their leader stated this: "There are two worlds that stand opposed to each other." And then in defiant reply to his opponents he said this: "Others are correct when they say: 'With this world we cannot ever reconcile ourselves.' I can beat any other power in the world." So said the leader of the Nazis.

In other words, the Axis not merely admits but the Axis proclaims that there can be no ultimate peace between their philosophy—their philosophy of government—and our philosophy of government.

In view of the nature of this undeniable threat, it can be asserted, properly and categorically, that the United States had no right or reason to encourage talk of peace until the day shall come when there is a clear intention on the part of the aggressor nations to abandon all thought of dominating or conquering the world.

At this moment the forces of the States that are leagued against all peoples who live in freedom are being held away from our shores. The Germans and the Italians are being blocked on the other side of the Atlantic by the British and by the Greeks, and by thousands of soldiers and sailors who were able to escape from subjugated countries. In Asia the Japanese are being engaged by the Chinese nation in another great defense.

In the Pacific Ocean is our fleet.

Some of our people like to believe that wars in Europe and Asia are of no concern to us. But it is a matter of most vital concern to us that European and Asiatic war-makers should not gain control of the oceans which lead to this hemisphere.

One hundred and seventeen years ago the Monroe Doctrine was conceived by our government as a measure of defense in the face of a threat against this hemisphere by an alliance in Continental Europe. Thereafter, we stood guard in the Atlantic, with the British as neighbors. There was no treaty. There was no "unwritten agreement."

And yet there was the feeling, proven correct by history, that we as neighbors could settle any disputes in peaceful fashion. And the fact is that during the whole of this time the Western Hemisphere has remained free from aggression from Europe or from Asia.

Does any one seriously believe that we need to fear attack anywhere in the Americas while a free Britain remains our most powerful naval neighbor in the Atlantic? And does any one seriously believe, on the other hand, that we could rest easy if the Axis powers were our neighbors there?

If Great Britain goes down, the Axis powers will control the Continents of Europe, Asia, Africa, Australia, and the high seas—and they will be in a position to bring enormous military and naval resources against this hemisphere. It is no exaggeration to say that all of us in all the Americas would be living at the point of a gun—a gun loaded with explosive bullets, economic as well as military.

We should enter upon a new and terrible era in which the whole world, our hemisphere included, would be run by threats of brute force. And to survive in such a world, we would have to convert ourselves permanently into a militaristic power on the basis of war economy.

Some of us like to believe that even if Britain falls, we are still safe, because of the broad expanse of the Atlantic and of the Pacific.

But the width of those oceans is not what it was in the days of clipper ships. At one point between Africa and Brazil the distance is less than it is from Washington to Denver, Colo., five hours for the latest type of bomber. And at the north end of the Pacific Ocean, America and Asia almost touch each other.

Why, even today we have planes that could fly from the British Isles to New England and back again without refueling. And remember that the range of the modern bomber is being ever increased.

During the past week many people in all parts of the nation have told me what they wanted me to say tonight. Almost all of them expressed a courageous desire to hear the plain truth about the gravity of the situation. One telegram, however, expressed the attitude of the small minority who want to see no evil and hear no evil, even though they know in their hearts that evil exists. That telegram begged me not to tell again of the ease with which our American cities could be bombed by any hostile power which had gained bases in this Western Hemisphere. The gist of that telegram was: "Please, Mr. President, don't frighten us by telling us the facts."

Frankly and definitely there is danger ahead—danger against which we must prepare. But we well know that we cannot escape danger, or the fear of danger, by crawling into bed and pulling the covers over our heads.

Some nations of Europe were bound by solemn non-intervention pacts with Germany. Other nations were assured by Germany that they need never fear invasion. Non-intervention pact or not, the fact remains that they were attacked, overrun, thrown into modern slavery at an hour's notice or even without any notice at all.

As an exiled leader of one of these nations said to me the other day, "The notice was a minus quantity. It was given to my government two hours after German troops had poured into my country in a hundred places." The fate of these nations tells us what it means to live at the point of a Nazi gun.

The Nazis have justified such actions by various pious frauds. One of these frauds is the claim that they are occupying a nation for the purpose of "restoring order." Another is that they are occupying or controlling a nation on the excuse that they are "protecting it" against the aggression of somebody else.

For example, Germany has said that she was occupying Belgium to save the Belgians from the British. Would she then hesitate to say to any South American country: "We are occupying you to protect you from aggression by the United States?"

Belgium today is being used as an invasion base against Britain, now fighting for its life. And any South American country, in Nazi hands, would always constitute a jumping off place for German attack on any one of the other republics of this hemisphere.

Analyze for yourselves the future of two other places even nearer to Germany if the Nazis won. Could Ireland hold out? Would Irish freedom be permitted as an amazing pet exception in an unfree world? Or the islands of the Azores, which still fly the flag of Portugal after five centuries? You and I think of Hawaii as an outpost of defense in the Pacific. And yet the Azores are closer to our shores in the Atlantic than Hawaii is on the other side.

There are those who say that the Axis powers would never have any desire to attack the Western Hemisphere. That is the same dangerous form of wishful thinking which has destroyed the powers of resistance of so many conquered peoples. The plain facts are that the Nazis have proclaimed, time and again, that all other races are their inferiors and therefore subject to their orders. And most important of all, the vast resources and wealth of this American hemisphere constitute the most tempting loot in all of the round world.

Let us no longer blind ourselves to the undeniable fact that the evil forces which have crushed and undermined and corrupted so many others are already within our own gates. Your government knows much about them and every day is ferreting them out.

Their secret emissaries are active in our own and in neighboring countries. They seek to stir up suspicion and dissension, to cause internal strife. They try to turn capital against labor, and vice versa. They try to reawaken long slumbering racial and religious enmities which should have no place in this country. They are active in every group that promotes intolerance. They exploit for their own ends our own natural abhorrence of war.

These trouble-breeders have but one purpose. It is to divide our people, to divide them into hostile groups and to destroy our unity and shatter our will to defend ourselves.

There are also American citizens, many of them in high places, who, unwittingly in most cases, are aiding and abetting the work of these agents. I do not charge these American citizens with being foreign agents. But I do charge them with doing exactly the kind of work that the dictators want done in the United States.

These people not only believe that we can save our own skins by shutting our eyes to the fate of other nations. Some of them go much further than that. They say that we can and should become the friends and even the partners of the Axis powers. Some of them even suggest that we should imitate the methods of the dictatorships. But Americans never can and never will do that.

The experience of the past two years has proven beyond doubt that no nation can appease the Nazis. No man can tame a tiger into a kitten by stroking it. There can be no appeasement with ruthlessness. There can be no reasoning with an incendiary bomb. We know now that a nation can have peace with the Nazis only at the price of total surrender.

Even the people of Italy have been forced to become accomplices of the Nazis; but at this moment they do not know how soon they will be embraced to death by their allies.

The American appeasers ignore the warning to be found in the fate of Austria, Czecho-Slovakia, Poland, Norway, Belgium, the Netherlands, Denmark and France. They tell you that the Axis powers are going to win anyway; that all of this bloodshed in the world could be saved, that the United States might just as well throw its influence into the scale of a dictated peace and get the best out of it that we can.

They call it a "negotiated peace." Nonsense! Is it a negotiated peace if a gang of outlaws surrounds your community and on threat of extermination makes you pay tribute to save your own skins?

Such a dictated peace would be no peace at all. It would be only another armistice, leading to the most gigantic armament race and the most devastating trade wars in all history. And in these contests the Americas would offer the only real resistance to the Axis powers. With all their vaunted efficiency, with all their parade of pious purpose in this war, there are still in their background the concentration camp and the servants of God in chains.

The history of recent years proves that the shootings and the chains and the concentration camps are not simply the transient tools but the very altars of modern dictatorships. They may talk of a "new order" in the world, but what they have in mind is only a revival of the oldest and worst tyranny. In that there is no liberty, no religion, no hope.

The proposed "new order" is the very opposite of a United States of Europe or a United States of Asia. It is not a government based upon the consent of the governed. It is not a union of ordinary, self-respecting men and women to protect themselves and their freedom and their dignity from oppression. It is an unholy alliance of power and pelf to dominate and enslave the human race.

The British people and their allies today are conducting an active war against this unholy alliance. Our own future security is greatly dependent on the outcome of that fight. Our ability to "keep out of war" is going to be affected by that outcome.

Thinking in terms of today and tomorrow, I make the direct statement to the American people that there is far less chance of the United States getting into war if we do all we can now to support the nations defending themselves against attack by the Axis than if we acquiesce in their defeat, submit tamely to an Axis victory, and wait our turn to be the object of attack in another war later on.

If we are to be completely honest with ourselves, we must admit that there is risk in any course we may take. But I deeply believe that the great majority of our people agree that the course that I advocate involves the least risk now and the greatest hope for world peace in the future.

The people of Europe who are defending themselves do not ask us to do their fighting. They ask us for the implements of war, the planes, the tanks, the guns, the freighters which will enable them to fight for their liberty and for our security. Emphatically we must get these weapons to them, get them to them in sufficient volume and quickly enough so that we and our children will be saved the agony and suffering of war which others have had to endure.

Let not the defeatists tell us that it is too late. It will never be earlier. Tomorrow will be later than today.

Certain facts are self-evident.

In a military sense Great Britain and the British Empire are today the spearhead of resistance to world conquest. And they are putting up a fight which will live forever in the story of human gallantry.

There is no demand for sending an American expeditionary force outside our own borders. There is not intention by any member of your government to send such a force. You can, therefore, nail, nail any talk about sending armies to Europe as deliberate untruth.

Our national policy is not directed toward war. Its sole purpose is to keep war away from our country and away from our people.

Democracy's fight against world conquest is being greatly aided, and must be more greatly aided, by the rearmament of the United States and by sending every ounce and every ton of munitions and supplies that we can possibly spare to help the defenders who are in the front lines. And it is no more unneutral for us to do that than it is for Sweden, Russia and other nations near Germany to send steel and ore and oil and other materials into Germany every day in the week.

We are planning our own defense with the utmost urgency, and in its vast scale we must integrate the war needs of Britain and the other free nations which are resisting aggression.

This is not a matter of sentiment or of controversial personal opinion. It is a matter of realistic, practical military policy, based on the advice of our military experts who are in close touch with existing warfare. These military and naval experts and the members of the Congress and the Administration have a single-minded purpose—the defense of the United States.

This nation is making a great effort to produce everything that is necessary in this emergency—and with all possible speed. And this great effort requires great sacrifice.

I would ask no one to defend a democracy which in turn would not defend every one in the nation against want and privation. The strength of this nation shall not be diluted by the failure of the government to protect the economic well-being of its citizens.

If our capacity to produce is limited by machines, it must ever be remembered that these machines are operated by the skill and the stamina of the workers. As the government is determined to protect the rights of the workers, so the nation has a right to expect that the men who man the machines will discharge their full responsibilities to the urgent needs of defense.

The worker possesses the same human dignity and is entitled to the same security of position as the engineer or the manager or the owner. For the workers provide the human power that turns out the destroyers, and the planes and the tanks.

The nation expects our defense industries to continue operation without interruption by strikes or lockouts. It expects and insists that management and workers will reconcile their differences by voluntary or legal means, to continue to produce the supplies that are so sorely needed.

And on the economic side of our great defense program, we are, as you know, bending every effort to maintain stability of prices and with that the stability of the cost of living.

Nine days ago I announced the setting up of a more effective organization to direct our gigantic efforts to increase the production of munitions. The appropriation of vast sums of money and a well-coordinated executive direction of our defense efforts are not in themselves enough. Guns, planes, ships and many other things have to be built in the factories and the arsenals of America. They have to be produced by workers and managers and engineers with the aid of machines which in turn have to be built by hundreds of thousands of workers throughout the land.

In this great work there has been splendid cooperation between the government and industry and labor. And I am very thankful.

American industrial genius, unmatched throughout all the world in the solution of production problems, has been called upon to bring its resources and its talents into action. Manufacturers of watches, of farm implements, of linotypes and cash registers and automobiles, and sewing machines and lawn mowers and locomotives, are now making fuses and bomb packing crates and telescope mounts and shells and pistols and tanks.

But all of our present efforts are not enough. We must have more ships, more guns, more planes—more of everything. And this can be accomplished only if we discard the notion of "business as usual." This job cannot be done merely by super-imposing on the existing productive facilities the added requirements of the nation for defense.

Our defense efforts must not be blocked by those who fear the future consequences of surplus plant capacity. The possible consequences of failure of our defense efforts now are much more to be feared.

And after the present needs of our defense are past, a proper handling of the country's peacetime needs will require all of the new productive capacity, if not still more.

No pessimistic policy about the future of America shall delay the immediate expansion of those industries essential to defense. We need them.

I want to make it clear that it is the purpose of the nation to build now with all possible speed every machine, every arsenal, every factory that we need to manufacture our defense material. We have the men—the skill—the wealth—and above all, the will.

I am confident that if and when production of consumer or luxury goods in certain industries requires the use of machines and raw materials that are essential for defense purposes, then such production must yield, and will gladly yield, to our primary and compelling purpose.

So I appeal to the owners of plants—to the managers—to the workers—to our own government employees—to put every ounce of effort into producing these munitions swiftly and without stint. With this appeal I give you the pledge that all of us who are officers of your government will devote ourselves to the same whole-hearted extent to the great task that lies ahead.

As planes and ships and guns and shells are produced, your government, with its defense experts, can then determine how best to use them to defend this hemisphere. The decision as to how much shall be sent abroad and how much shall remain at home must be made on the basis of our over-all military necessities.

We must be the great arsenal of democracy. For us this is an emergency as serious as war itself. We must apply ourselves to our task with the same resolution, the same sense of urgency, the same spirit of patriotism and sacrifice as we would show were we at war.

We have furnished the British great material support and we will furnish far more in the future.

There will be no "bottlenecks" in our determination to aid Great Britain. No dictator, no combination of dictators, will weaken that determination by threats of how they will construe that determination.

The British have received invaluable military support from the heroic Greek army and from the forces of all the governments in exile. Their strength is growing. It is the strength of men and women who value their freedom more highly than they value their lives.

I believe that the Axis powers are not going to win this war. I base that belief on the latest and best of information.

We have no excuse for defeatism. We have every good reason for hope—hope for peace, yes, and hope for the defense of our civilization and for the building of a better civilization in the future.

I have the profound conviction that the American people are now determined to put forth a mightier effort than they have ever yet made to increase our production of all the implements of defense, to meet the threat of our democratic faith.

As President of the United States, I call for that national effort. I call for it in the name of this nation which we love and honor and which we are privileged and proud to serve. I call upon our people with absolute confidence that our common cause will greatly succeed.

State of the Union Message to Congress
("The Four Freedoms")
Washington, D.C., January 6, 1941

The military-political context of the debate over Lend-Lease in the winter of 1940-41 was the Battle of Britain raging night after night in the sky above England, with reports from the scene of that conflict appearing every day in American newspapers and newsreels. There is little question that sympathy with the British in this vital struggle for survival aided the fight for public opinion in support of Lend-Lease in America. Whatever may have been his private thoughts on the matter—many historians have written what now seems obvious, that by this time FDR could hardly have still believed that the Axis powers could be overthrown without the direct military intervention of the United States—he was still able to argue that making war materiel available to the British through Lend-Lease was the only way to avoid sending American soldiers to fight overseas. Winston Churchill got on the same bandwagon during this debate when in a broadcast to America he simply promised, "Give us the tools and we will finish the job." The American public largely agreed, and after a few months of debate, Lend-Lease passed Congress by healthy majorities: 260 to 165 in the House, 60 to 31 in the Senate.

On January 6, 1941, the week after his "Arsenal of Democracy" Fireside Chat, while the Lend-Lease debate was in its early stages, Roosevelt delivered his State of the Union message to Congress. In it, he reiterated his position on the need to aid the world's democracies in the struggle against fascism, and beyond that, outlined the philosophical basis of his position as head of a nation confronting the possibility of world war: "In future days," he said, "which we seek to make secure, we look forward to a world founded upon four essential human freedoms." These were freedom of speech, freedom of worship, freedom from want, and freedom from fear. It was reported that applause in Congress was strong but somewhat subdued, not because anyone disagreed with the idea of the "Four Freedoms"—as this philosophical program became known—but because FDR's words had brought home to his audience the gravity of the situation at that moment.

Mr. Speaker, members of the 77th Congress:

I address you, the members of this new Congress, at a moment unprecedented in the history of the union. I use the word "unprecedented" because at no previous time has American security been as seriously threatened from without as it is today.

Since the permanent formation of our government under the Constitution in 1789, most of the periods of crisis in our history have related to our domestic affairs. And, fortunately, only one of these—the four-year war between the States—ever threatened our national unity. Today, thank God, 130,000,000 Americans in forty-eight States have forgotten points of the compass in our national unity.

It is true that prior to 1914 the United States often has been disturbed by events in other continents. We have even engaged in two wars with European nations and in a number of undeclared wars in the West Indies, in the Mediterranean and in the Pacific, for the maintenance of American rights and for the Principles of peaceful commerce. But in no case has a serious threat been raised against our national safety or our continued independence.

What I seek to convey is the historic truth that the United States as a nation has at all times maintained opposition—clear, definite opposition—to any attempt to lock us in behind an ancient Chinese wall while the procession of civilization went past. Today, thinking of our children and of their children, we oppose enforced isolation for ourselves or for any other part of the Americas.

That determination of ours, extending over all these years, was proved, for example, in the early days during the quarter century of wars following the French Revolution. While the Napoleonic struggle did threaten interests of the United States because of the French foothold in the West Indies and in Louisiana, and while we engaged in the War of 1812 to vindicate our right to peaceful trade, it is nevertheless clear that neither France nor Great Britain nor any other nation was aiming at domination of the whole world.

And in like fashion, from 1815 to 1914—ninety-nine years—no single war in Europe or in Asia constituted a real threat against our future or against the future of any other American nation.

Except in the Maximilian interlude in Mexico, no foreign power sought to establish itself in this hemisphere. And the strength of the British fleet in the Atlantic has been a friendly strength; it is still a friendly strength. Even when the World War broke out in 1914 it seemed to contain only small threat of danger to our own American future. But as time went on, as we remember, the American people began to visualize what the downfall of democratic nations might mean to our own democracy.

We need not overemphasize imperfections in the peace of Versailles. We need not harp on failure of the democracies to deal with problems of world reconstruction. We should remember that the peace of 1919 was far less unjust than the kind of pacification which began even before Munich, and which is being carried on under the new order of tyranny that seeks to spread over every continent today. The American people have unalterably set their faces against that tyranny. I suppose that every realist knows that the democratic way of life is at this moment being directly assailed in every part of the world—assailed either by arms or by secret spreading of poisionous propaganda by those who seek to destroy unity and promote discord in nations that are still at peace.

During sixteen long months this assault has blotted out the whole pattern of democratic life in an appalling number of independent nations, great and small. And the assailants are still on the march, threatening other nations, great and small. Therefore, as your President, performing my constitutional duty to "give to the Congress information of the state of the union," I find it unhappily necessary to report that the future and the safety of our country and of our democracy are overwhelmingly involved in events far beyond our borders.

Armed defense of democratic existence is now being gallantly waged in four continents. If that defense fails, all the population and all the resources of Europe and Asia, Africa and Australia will be dominated by conquerors. And let us remember that the total of those populations in those four continents, the total of those populations and their resources greatly exceeds the sum total of the population and the resources of the whole of the Western Hemisphere—yes, many times over.

In times like these it is immature—and, incidentally, untrue—for anybody to brag that an unprepared America, single-handed and with one hand tied behind its back, can hold off the whole world. No realistic American can expect from a dictator's peace international generosity, or return of true independence, or world disarmament, or freedom of expression, or freedom of religion—or even good business. Such a peace would bring no security for us or for our neighbors. Those who would give up essential liberty to purchase a little temporary safety deserve neither liberty nor safety.

As a nation we may take pride in the fact that we are soft-hearted; but we cannot afford to be soft-headed. We must always be wary of those who with sounding brass and a tinkling cymbal preach the ism of appeasement. We must especially beware of that small group of selfish men who would clip the wings of the American eagle in order to feather their own nests. I have recently pointed out how quickly the tempo of modern warfare could bring into our very midst the physical attack which we must eventually expect if the dictator nations win this war.

There is much loose talk of our immunity from immediate and direct invasion from across the seas. Obviously, as long as the British Navy retains its power, no such danger exists. Even if there were no British Navy, it is not probable that any enemy would be stupid enough to attack us by landing troops in the United States from across thousands of miles of ocean, until it had acquired strategic bases from which to operate. But we learn much from the lessons of the past years in Europe—particularly the lesson of Norway, whose essential seaports were captured by treachery and surprise built up over a series of years.

The first phase of the invasion of this hemisphere would not be the landing of regular troops. The necessary strategic points would be occupied by secret agents and by their dupes—and great numbers of them are already here and in Latin America. As long as the aggressor nations maintain the offensive they, not we, will choose the time and the place and the method of their attack. And that is why the future of all the American Republics is today in serious danger. That is why this annual message to the Congress is unique in our history. That is why every member of the executive branch of the government and every member of the Congress face great responsibility—great accountability.

The need of the moment is that our actions and our policy should be devoted primarily—almost exclusively—to meeting this foreign peril. For all our domestic problems are now a part of the great emergency. Just as our national policy in internal affairs has been based upon a decent respect for the rights and the dignity of all of our fellow men within our gates, so our national policy in foreign affairs has been based on a decent respect for the rights and the dignity of all nations, large and small. And the justice of morality must and will win in the end.

Our national policy is this: First, by an impressive expression of the public will and without regard to partisanship, we are committed to all-inclusive national defense. Second, by an impressive expression of the public will and without regard to partisanship, we are committed to full support of all those resolute people everywhere who are resisting aggression and are thereby keeping war away from our hemisphere. By this support we express our determination that the democratic cause shall prevail, and we strengthen the defense and the security of our own nation.

Third, by an impressive expression of the public will and without regard to partisanship, we are committed to the proposition that principle of morality and considerations for our own security will never permit us to acquiesce in a peace dictated by aggressors and sponsored by appeasers. We know that enduring peace cannot be bought at the cost of other people's freedom. In the recent national election there was no substantial difference between the two great parties in respect to that national policy. No issue was fought out on the line before the American electorate. And today it is abundantly evident that American citizens everywhere are demanding and supporting speedy and complete action in recognition of obvious danger.

Therefore, the immediate need is a swift and driving increase in our armament production. Leaders of industry and labor have responded to our summons. Goals of speed have been set. In some cases these goals are being reached ahead of time. In some cases we are on schedule; in other cases there are slight but not serious delays. And in some cases — and, I am sorry to say, very important cases — we are all concerned by the slowness of the accomplishment of our plans. The Army and Navy, however, have made substantial progress during the past year. Actual experience is improving and speeding up our methods of production with every passing day. And today's best is not good enough for tomorrow.

I am not satisfied with the progress thus far made. The men in charge of the program represent the best in training, in ability and in patriotism. They are not satisfied with the progress thus far made. None of us will be satisfied until the job is done. No matter whether the original goal was set too high or too low, our objective is quicker and better results. To give you two illustrations: We are behind schedule in turning out finished airplanes. We are working day and night to solve the innumerable problems and to catch up.

We are ahead of schedule in building warships, but we are working to get even further ahead of that schedule. To change a whole nation from a basis of peacetime production of implements of peace to a basis of wartime production of implements of war is no small task. The greatest difficulty comes at the beginning of the program, when new tools, new plant facilities, new assembly lines, new shipways must first be constructed before the actual material begins to flow steadily and speedily from them.

The Congress of course, must rightly keep itself informed at all times of the progress of the program. However, there is certain information, as the Congress itself will readily recognize, which, in the interests of our own security and those of the nations that we are supporting, must of needs be kept in confidence. New circumstances are constantly begetting new needs for our safety. I shall ask this Congress for greatly increased new appropriations and authorizations to carry on what we have begun.

I also ask this Congress for authority and for funds sufficient to manufacture additional munitions and war supplies of many kinds, to be turned over to those nations which are now in actual war with aggressor nations. Our most useful and immediate role is to act as an arsenal for them as well as for ourselves. They do not need manpower, but they do need billions of dollars' worth of the weapons of defense. The time is near when they will not be able to pay for them all in ready cash. We cannot, and we will not, tell them that they must surrender merely because of present inability to pay for the weapons which we know they must have.

I do not recommend that we make them a loan of dollars with which to pay for these weapons—a loan to be repaid in dollars. I recommend that we make it possible for those nations to continue to obtain war materials in the United States, fitting their orders into our own program. And nearly all of their material would, if the time ever came, be useful in our own defense. Taking counsel of expert military and naval authorities, considering what is best for our own security, we are free to decide how much should be kept here and how much should be sent abroad to our friends who, by their determined and heroic resistance, are giving us time in which to make ready our own defense.

For what we send abroad we shall be repaid, repaid within a reasonable time following the close of hostilities, repaid in similar materials, or at our option in other goods of many kinds which they can produce and which we need. Let us say to the democracies: "We Americans are vitally concerned in your defense of freedom. We are putting forth our energies, our resources and our organizing powers to give you the strength to regain and maintain a free world. We shall send you in ever-increasing numbers, ships, planes, tanks, guns. That is our purpose and our pledge."

In fulfillment of this purpose we will not be intimidated by the threats of dictators that they will regard as a breach of international law or as an act of war our aid to the democracies which dare to resist their aggression. Such aid is not an act of war, even if a dictator should unilaterally proclaim it so to be.

And when the dictators—if the dictators—are ready to make war upon us, they will not wait for an act of war on our part.

They did not wait for Norway or Belgium or the Netherlands to commit an act of war. Their only interest is in a new one-way international law which lacks mutuality in its observance and therefore becomes an instrument of oppression. The happiness of future generations of Americans may well depend on how effective and how immediate we can make our aid felt. No one can tell the exact character of the emergency situations that we may be called upon to meet. The nation's hands must not be tied when the nation's life is in danger.

Yes, and we must prepare, all of us prepare, to make the sacrifices that the emergency—almost as serious as war itself—demands. Whatever stands in the way of speed and efficiency in defense, in defense preparations at any time, must give way to the national need.

A free nation has the right to expect full cooperation from all groups. A free nation has the right to look to the leaders of business, of labor and of agriculture to take the lead in stimulating effort, not among other groups but within their own groups.

The best way of dealing with the few slackers or trouble-makers in our midst is, first, to shame them by patriotic example, and if that fails, to use the sovereignty of government to save government.

As men do not live by bread alone, they do not fight by armaments alone. Those who man our defenses and those behind them who build our defenses must have the stamina and the courage which come from unshakeable belief in the manner of life which they are defending. The mighty action that we are calling for cannot be based on a disregard of all the things worth fighting for.

The nation takes great satisfaction and much strength from the things which have been done to make its people conscious of their individual stake in the preservation of democratic life in America. Those things have toughened the fiber of our people, have renewed their faith and strengthened their devotion to the institutions we make ready to protect. Certainly this is no time for any of us to stop thinking about the social and economic problems which are the root cause of the social revolution which is today a supreme factor in the world. For there is nothing mysterious about the foundations of a healthy and strong democracy.

The basic things expected by our people of their political and economic systems are simple. They are:

Equality of opportunity for youth and for others.

Jobs for those who can work.

Security for those who need it.

The ending of special privilege for the few.

The preservation of civil liberties for all.

The enjoyment of the fruits of scientific progress in a wider and constantly rising standard of living.

These are the simple, the basic things that must never be lost sight of in the turmoil and unbelievable complexity of our modern world. The inner and abiding strength of our economic and political systems is dependent upon the degree to which they fulfill these expectations. Many subjects connected with our social economy call for immediate improvement. As examples:

We should bring more citizens under the coverage of old-age pensions and unemployment insurance.

We should widen the opportunities for adequate medical care.

We should plan a better system by which persons deserving or needing gainful employment may obtain it.

I have called for personal sacrifice, and I am assured of the willingness of almost all Americans to respond to that call. A part of the sacrifice means the payment of more money in taxes. In my budget message I will recommend that a greater portion of this great defense program be paid for from taxation than we are paying for today. No person should try, or be allowed to get rich out of the program, and the principle of tax payments in accordance with ability to pay should be constantly before our eyes to guide our legislation.

If the congress maintains these principles the voters, putting patriotism ahead of pocketbooks, will give you their applause.

In the future days which we seek to make secure, we look forward to a world founded upon four essential human freedoms.

The first is freedom of speech and expression—everywhere in the world.

The second is freedom of every person to worship God in his own way—everywhere in the world.

The third is freedom from want, which, translated into world terms, means economic understandings which will secure to every nation a healthy peacetime life for its inhabitants—everywhere in the world.

The fourth is freedom from fear, which, translated into world terms, means a world-wide reduction of armaments to such a point and in such a thorough fashion that no nation will be in a position to commit an act of physical aggression against any neighbor—anywhere in the world.

That is no vision of a distant millennium. It is a definite basis for a kind of world attainable in our own time and generation. That kind of world is the very antithesis of the so-called "new order" of tyranny which the dictators seek to create with the crash of a bomb.

To that new order we oppose the greater conception—the moral order. A good society is able to face schemes of world domination and foreign revolutions alike without fear. Since the beginning of our American history we have been engaged in change, in a perpetual, peaceful revolution, a revolution which goes on steadily, quietly, adjusting itself to changing conditions without the concentration camp or the quicklime in the ditch. The world order which we seek is the cooperation of free countries, working together in a friendly, civilized society.

This nation has placed its destiny in the hands, heads and hearts of its millions of free men and women, and its faith in freedom under the guidance of God. Freedom means the supremacy of human rights everywhere. Our support goes to those who struggle to gain those rights and keep them. Our strength is our unity of purpose.

To that high concept there can be no end save victory.

Third Inaugural Address
Washington, D.C., January 20, 1941

Roosevelt's campaign for a third term was dominated by two issues, the debate over isolationism and Republican charges that
FDR's policies would bring the country into war, and his unprecedented third term election bid. His opponent, Wendell
Wilkie, was a respected moderate Republican who held many
views that were close to Roosevelt's own, as well as a skilled campaigner. FDR was uneasy about the outcome of the election, convinced at the end that he would win, but only by a narrow margin
that might not give him a sufficient mandate for obtaining the increased aid to Britain and other nations then at war with the
Nazis. Ultimately, the election was closer than the first two, but
not as close as Roosevelt had himself predicted. He won with 25
million popular votes to 22 million for Wilkie, and 449 to 82 in
the electoral college. His Third Inaugural Address came two
weeks after the momentous "Four Freedoms" message to
Congress, and was in itself a thoughtful and solemn interpretation
of the meaning of American democracy.

On each national day of inauguration since 1789, the people have renewed their sense of dedication to the United States.

In Washington's day the task of the people was to create and weld together a nation.

In Lincoln's day the task of the people was to preserve that Nation
from disruption from within.

In this day the task of the people is to save that Nation and its institutions from disruption from without.

To us there has come a time, in the midst of swift happenings, to
pause for a moment and take stock—to recall what our place in history
has been, and to rediscover what we are and what we may be. If we do
not, we risk the real peril of inaction.

Lives of nations are determined not by the count of years, but by the lifetime of the human spirit. The life of a man is three-score years and ten: a little more, a little less. The life of a nation is the fullness of the measure of its will to live.

There are men who doubt this. There are men who believe that democracy, as a form of Government and a frame of life, is limited or measured by a kind of mystical and artificial fate, that for some unexplained reason, tyranny and slavery have become the surging wave of the future—and that freedom is an ebbing tide.

But we Americans know that this is not true.

Eight years ago, when the life of this Republic seemed frozen by a fatalistic terror, we proved that this is not true. We were in the midst of shock—but we acted. We acted quickly, boldly, decisively.

These later years have been living years—fruitful years for the people of this democracy. For they have brought to us greater security and, I hope, a better understanding that life's ideals are to be measured in other than material things.

Most vital to our present and our future is this experience of a democracy which successfully survived crisis at home; put away many evil things; built new structures on enduring lines; and, through it all, maintained the fact of its democracy.

For action has been taken within the three-way framework of the Constitution of the United States. The coordinate branches of the Government continue freely to function. The Bill of Rights remains inviolate. The freedom of elections is wholly maintained. Prophets of the downfall of American democracy have seen their dire predictions come to naught.

Democracy is not dying.

We know it because we have seen it revive—and grow.

We know it cannot die—because it is built on the unhampered initiative of individual men and women joined together in a common enterprise—an enterprise undertaken and carried through by the free expression of a free majority.

We know it because democracy alone, of all forms of government, enlists the full force of men's enlightened will.

We know it because democracy alone has constructed an unlimited civilization capable of infinite progress in the improvement of human life.

We know it because, if we look below the surface, we sense it still spreading on every continent—for it is the most humane, the most advanced, and in the end the most unconquerable of all forms of human society.

A nation, like a person, has a body—a body that must be fed and clothed and housed, invigorated and rested, in a manner that measures up to the objectives of our time.

A nation, like a person, has a mind—a mind that must be kept informed and alert, that must know itself, that understands the hopes and the needs of its neighbors—all the other nations that live within the narrowing circle of the world.

And a nation, like a person, has something deeper, something more permanent, something larger than the sum of all its parts. It is that something which matters most to its future—which calls forth the most sacred guarding of its present.

It is a thing for which we find it difficult—even impossible—to hit upon a single, simple word.

And yet we all understand what it is—the spirit—the faith of America. It is the product of centuries. It was born in the multitudes of those who came from many lands—some of high degree, but mostly plain people, who sought here, early and late, to find freedom more freely.

The democratic aspiration is no mere recent phase in human history. It is human history. It permeated the ancient life of early peoples. It blazed anew in the middle ages. It was written in Magna Carta.

In the Americas its impact has been irresistible. America has been the New World in all tongues, to all peoples, not because this continent was a new-found land, but because all those who came here believed they could create upon this continent a new life—a life that should be new in freedom.

Its vitality was written into our own Mayflower Compact, into the Declaration of Independence, into the Constitution of the United States, into the Gettysburg Address.

Those who first came here to carry out the longings of their spirit, and the millions who followed, and the stock that sprang from them—all have moved forward constantly and consistently toward an ideal which in itself has gained stature and clarity with each generation.

The hopes of the Republic cannot forever tolerate either undeserved poverty or self-serving wealth.

We know that we still have far to go; that we must more greatly build the security and the opportunity and the knowledge of every citizen, in the measure justified by the resources and the capacity of the land.

But it is not enough to achieve these purposes alone. It is not enough to clothe and feed the body of this Nation, and instruct and inform its mind. For there is also the spirit. And of the three, the greatest is the spirit.

Without the body and the mind, as all men know, the Nation could not live.

But if the spirit of America were killed, even though the Nation's body and mind, constricted in an alien world, lived on, the America we know would have perished.

That spirit—that faith—speaks to us in our daily lives in ways often unnoticed, because they seem so obvious. It speaks to us here in the Capital of the Nation. It speaks to us through the processes of governing in the sovereignties of 48 States. It speaks to us in our counties, in our cities, in our towns, and in our villages. It speaks to us from the other nations of the hemisphere, and from those across the seas—the enslaved, as well as the free. Sometimes we fail to hear or heed these voices of freedom because to us the privilege of our freedom is such an old, old story.

The destiny of America was proclaimed in words of prophecy spoken by our first President in his first inaugural in 1789—words almost directed, it would seem, to this year of 1941: "The preservation of the sacred fire of liberty and the destiny of the republican model of government are justly considered . . . deeply, . . . finally, staked on the experiment intrusted to the hands of the American people."

If we lose that sacred fire—if we let it be smothered with doubt and fear—then we shall reject the destiny which Washington strove so valiantly and so triumphantly to establish. The preservation of the spirit and faith of the Nation does, and will, furnish the highest justification for every sacrifice that we may make in the cause of national defense.

In the face of great perils never before encountered, our strong purpose is to protect and to perpetuate the integrity of democracy.

For this we muster the spirit of America, and the faith of America.

We do not retreat. We are not content to stand still. As Americans, we go forward, in the service of our country, by the will of God.

Fireside Chat (on German submarine attacks)
Washington, D.C., September 11, 1941*

While the Japanese attack on Pearl Harbor on December 7, 1941 was the event which officially propelled America into World War II, the decisive incident could just as easily have derived from the long, bitter, undeclared quasi-war between the American and German navies in the Atlantic. There were many shooting incidents in the twenty-seven months between Germany's invasion of Poland and the attack on Pearl Harbor—a major one the attack by a German U-boat on an American destroyer, the U.S.S. *Greer*, southeast of Greenland on September 4, 1941. To rally public support for a more militant policy against the depredations of the German navy in the Atlantic, the account which FDR gave of the *Greer* incident in this Fireside Chat on September 11, 1941 was highly colored. A British bomber was also in the area dropping depth charges, and the German submarine commander may not have been sure whether the destroyer was English or American, or exactly where the depth charges were coming from; but the attack served FDR's purposes in the ongoing debate over modification of the Neutrality Act. FDR used the *Greer* incident as justification to give orders to American naval commanders to "shoot on sight" at German and Italian submarines, and other military vessels south and west of Iceland.

The *Greer* itself had not actually been damaged in the September 4th episode; but while the public was digesting the news of that event, another German submarine struck on October 16th, attacking an American convoy and torpedoing another American destroyer—the U.S.S. *Kearny*—this time with the loss of eleven American lives. Public opinion rallied behind FDR's new policy on attacking Nazi submarines, and solidified two weeks later when a third American destroyer, the *Reuben James*, was sunk while protecting another convoy, this time with the loss

*This Fireside Chat was originally scheduled for September 8th, but was delayed for three days by the death of FDR's mother on that date while he was visiting Hyde Park.

of over a hundred American sailors. By the time Pearl Harbor brought America into the war in the Pacific a month later, the country was in effect already at war with Germany in the North Atlantic.

My Fellow Americans:

The Navy Department of the United States has reported to me that on the morning of September fourth the United States destroyer *Greer*, proceeding in full daylight towards Iceland, had reached a point southeast of Greenland. She was carrying American mail to Iceland. She was flying the American flag. Her identity as an American ship was unmistakable.

She was then and there attacked by a submarine. Germany admits that it was a German submarine. The submarine deliberately fired a torpedo at the *Greer*, followed later by another torpedo attack. In spite of what Hitler's propaganda bureau has invented, and in spite of what any American obstructionist organization may prefer to believe, I tell you the blunt fact that the German submarine fired first upon this American destroyer without warning, and with deliberate design to sink her.

Our destroyer, at the time, was in waters which the Government of the United States had declared to be waters of self-defense—surrounding outposts of American protection in the Atlantic.

In the North of the Atlantic, outposts have been established by us in Iceland, in Greenland, in Labrador and in Newfoundland. Through these waters there pass many ships of many flags. They bear food and other supplies to civilians; and they bear material of war, for which the people of the United States are spending billions of dollars, and which, by Congressional action, they have declared to be essential for the defense of our own land.

The United States destroyer, when attacked, was proceeding on a legitimate mission.

If the destroyer was visible to the submarine when the torpedo was fired, then the attack was a deliberate attempt by the Nazis to sink a clearly identified American warship. On the other hand, if the submarine was beneath the surface of the sea and, with the aid of its listening devices, fired in the direction of the sound of the American destroyer without even taking the trouble to learn its identity—as the official German communique would indicate—then the attack was even more outrageous. For it indicates a policy of indiscriminate violence against any vessel sailing the seas—belligerent or non-belligerent.

This was piracy—piracy legally and morally. It was not the first nor the last act of piracy which the Nazi Government has committed against the American flag in this war. For attack has followed attack.

A few months ago an American flag merchant ship, the *Robin Moor*, was sunk by a Nazi submarine in the middle of the South Atlantic, under circumstances violating long-established international law and violating every principle of humanity. The passengers and the crew were forced into open boats hundreds of miles from land, in direct violation of international agreements signed by nearly all nations including the Government of Germany. No apology, no allegation of mistake, no offer of reparations has come from the Nazi Government.

In July, 1941, nearly two months ago an American battleship in North American waters was followed by a submarine which for a long time sought to maneuver itself into a position of attack upon the battleship. The periscope of the submarine was clearly seen. No British or American submarines were within hundreds of miles of this spot at the time, so the nationality of the submarine is clear.

Five days ago a United States Navy ship on patrol picked up three survivors of an American-owned ship operating under the flag of our sister Republic of Panama — the S.S. *Sessa*. On August seventeenth, she had been first torpedoed without warning, and then shelled, near Greenland, while carrying civilian supplies to Iceland. It is feared that the other members of her crew have been drowned. In view of the established presence of German submarines in this vicinity, there can be no reasonable doubt as to the identity of the flag of the attacker.

Five days ago, another United States merchant ship, the *Steel Seafarer*, was sunk by a German aircraft in the Red Sea two hundred and twenty miles south of Suez. She was bound for an Egyptian port.

So four of the vessels sunk or attacked flew the American flag and were clearly identifiable. Two of these ships were warships of the American Navy. In the fifth case, the vessel sunk clearly carried the flag of our sister Republic of Panama.

In the face of all this, we Americans are keeping our feet on the ground. Our type of democratic civilization has outgrown the thought of feeling compelled to fight some other nation by reason of any single piratical attack on one of our ships. We are not becoming hysterical or losing our sense of proportion. Therefore, what I am thinking and saying tonight does not relate to any isolated episode.

Instead, we Americans are taking a long-range point of view in regard to certain fundamentals — a point of view in regard to a series of events on land and on sea which must be considered as a whole — as a part of a world pattern.

It would be unworthy of a great nation to exaggerate an isolated incident, or to become inflamed by some one act of violence. But it would be inexcusable folly to minimize such incidents in the face of evidence which makes it clear that the incident is not isolated, but is part of a general plan.

The important truth is that these acts of international lawlessness are a manifestation of a design—a design that has been made clear to the American people for a long time. It is the Nazi design to abolish the freedom of the seas, and to acquire absolute control and domination of these seas for themselves.

For with control of the seas in their own hands, the way can obviously become clear for their next step—domination of the United States—domination of the Western Hemisphere by force of arms. Under Nazi control of the seas, no merchant ship of the United States or of any other American Republic would be free to carry on any peaceful commerce, except by the condescending grace of this foreign and tyrannical power. The Atlantic Ocean which has been, and which should always be, a free and friendly highway for us would then become a deadly menace to the commerce of the United States, to the coasts of the United States, and even to the inland cities of the United States.

The Hitler Government, in defiance of the laws of the sea, in defiance of the recognized rights of all other nations, has presumed to declare, on paper, that great areas of the seas—even including a vast expanse lying in the Western Hemisphere—are to be closed, and that no ships may enter them for any purpose, except at peril of being sunk. Actually they are sinking ships at will and without warning in widely separated areas both within and far outside of these far-flung pretended zones.

This Nazi attempt to seize control of the oceans is but a counterpart of the Nazi plots now being carried on throughout the Western Hemisphere—all designed toward the same end. For Hitler's advance guards—not only his avowed agents but also his dupes among us— have sought to make ready for him footholds, bridgeheads in the New World, to be used as soon as he has gained control of the oceans.

His intrigues, his plots, his machinations, his sabotage in this New World are all known to the Government of the United States. Conspiracy has followed conspiracy. For example, last year a plot to seize the Government of Uruguay was smashed by the prompt action of that country, which was supported in full by her American neighbors. A like plot was then hatching in Argentina, and that government has carefully and wisely blocked it at every point. More recently, an endeavor was made to subvert the government of Bolivia. And within the past few weeks the discovery was made of secret air-landing fields in Colombia, within easy range of the Panama Canal. I could multiply instance upon instance.

To be ultimately successful in world mastery, Hitler knows that he must get control of the seas. He must first destroy the bridge of ships which we are building across the Atlantic and over which we shall continue to roll the implements of war to help destroy him, to destroy all his works in the end. He must wipe out our patrol on sea and in the air if he is to do it. He must silence the British Navy.

I think it must be explained over and over again to people who like to think of the United States Navy as an invincible protection, that this can be true only if the British Navy survives. And that, my friends, is simple arithmetic.

For if the world outside of the Americas falls under Axis domination, the shipbuilding facilities which the Axis powers would then possess in all of Europe, in the British Isles and in the Far East would be much greater than all the shipbuilding facilities and potentialities of all of the Americas—not only greater, but two or three times greater, enough to win. Even if the United States threw all its resources into such a situation, seeking to double and even redouble the size of our Navy, the Axis powers, in control of the rest of the world, would have the manpower and the physical resources to outbuild us several times over.

It is time for all Americans, Americans of all the Americas to stop being deluded by the romantic notion that the Americas can go on living happily and peacefully in a Nazi-dominated world.

Generation after generation, America has battled for the general policy of the freedom of the seas. And that policy is a very simple one, but a basic, a fundamental one. It means that no nation has the right to make the broad oceans of the world at great distances from the actual theatre of land war, unsafe for the commerce of others. That has been our policy, proved time and again, in all of our history. Our policy has applied from the earliest days of the Republic—and still applies—not merely to the Atlantic but to the Pacific and to all other oceans as well.

Unrestricted submarine warfare in 1941 constitutes a defiance—an act of aggression—against that historic American policy.

It is now clear that Hitler has begun his campaign to control the seas by ruthless force and by wiping out every vestige of international law, every vestige of humanity.

His intention has been made clear. The American people can have no further illusions about it.

No tender whisperings of appeasers that Hitler is not interested in the Western Hemisphere, no soporific lullabies that a wide ocean protects us from him—can long have any effect on the hard-headed, farsighted and realistic American people.

Because of these episodes, because of the movements and operations of German warships, and because of the clear, repeated proof that the present government of Germany has no respect for treaties or for international law, that it has no decent attitude toward neutral nations or human life—we Americans are now face to face not with abstract theories but with cruel, relentless facts.

This attack on the *Greer* was no localized military operation in the North Atlantic. This was no mere episode in a struggle between two nations. This was one determined step towards creating a permanent world system based on force, on terror and on murder.

And I am sure that even now the Nazis are waiting, waiting to see whether the United States will by silence give them the green light to go ahead on this path of destruction.

The Nazi danger to our Western world has long ceased to be a mere possibility. The danger is here now—not only from a military enemy but from an enemy of all law, all liberty, all morality, all religion.

There has now come a time when you and I must see the cold inexorable necessity of saying to these inhuman, unrestrained seekers of world conquest and permanent world domination by the sword: "You seek to throw our children and our children's children into your form of terrorism and slavery. You have now attacked our own safety. You shall go no further."

Normal practices of diplomacy—note writing—are of no possible use in dealing with international outlaws who sink our ships and kill our citizens.

One peaceful nation after another has met disaster because each refused to look the Nazi danger squarely in the eye until it had actually had them by the throat.

The United States will not make that fatal mistake.

No act of violence, no act of intimidation will keep us from maintaining intact two bulwarks of American defense: First, our line of supply of material to the enemies of Hitler; and second, the freedom of our shipping on the high seas.

No matter what it takes, no matter what it costs, we will keep open the line of legitimate commerce in these defensive waters of ours.

We have sought no shooting war with Hitler. We do not seek it now. But neither do we want peace so much, that we are willing to pay for it by permitting him to attack our naval and merchant ships while they are on legitimate business.

I assume that the German leaders are not deeply concerned, tonight or any other time, by what we Americans or the American Government say or publish about them. We cannot bring about the downfall of Nazi-ism by the use of long-range invective. But when you see a rattlesnake poised to strike, you do not wait until he has struck before you crush him.

These Nazi submarines and raiders are the rattlesnakes of the Atlantic. They are a menace to the free pathways of the high seas. They are a challenge to our own sovereignty. They hammer at our most precious rights when they attack ships of the American flag—symbols of our independence, our freedom, our very life.

It is clear to all Americans that the time has come when the Americas themselves must now be defended. A continuation of attacks in our own waters or in waters that could be used for further and greater attacks on us, will inevitably weaken our American ability to repel Hitlerism.

Do not let us be hair-splitters. Let us not ask ourselves whether the Americas should begin to defend themselves after the first attack, or the fifth attack, or the tenth attack, or the twentieth attack.

The time for active defense is now.

Do not let us be hair-splitters. Let us not say: "We will only defend ourselves if the torpedo succeeds in getting home, or if the crew and the passengers are drowned." This is the time for prevention of attack.

If submarines or raiders attack in distant waters, they can attack equally well within sight of our own shores. Their very presence in any waters which America deems vital to its defense constitutes an attack.

In the waters which we deem necessary for our defense, American naval vessels and American planes will no longer wait until Axis submarines lurking under the water, or Axis raiders on the surface of the sea, strike their deadly blow—first.

Upon our naval and air patrol—now operating in large number over a vast expanse of the Atlantic Ocean—falls the duty of maintaining the American policy of freedom of the seas—now. That means, very simply, very clearly, that our patrolling vessels and planes will protect all merchant ships—not only American ships but ships of any flag—engaged in commerce in our defensive waters. They will protect them from submarines; they will protect them from surface raiders.

This situation is not new. The second President of the United States, John Adams, ordered the United States Navy to clean out European privateers and European ships of war which were infesting the Caribbean and South American waters, destroying American commerce.

The third President of the United States, Thomas Jefferson, ordered the United States Navy to end the attacks being made upon American and other ships by the corsairs of the nations of North Africa.

My obligation as President is historic; it is clear. Yes, it is inescapable.

It is no act of war on our part when we decide to protect the seas that are vital to American defense. The aggression is not ours. Ours is solely defense.

But let this warning be clear. From now on, if German or Italian vessels of war enter the waters, the protection of which is necessary for American defense, they do so at their own peril.

The orders which I have given as Commander-in-Chief of the United States Army and Navy are to carry out that policy—at once.

The sole responsibility rests upon Germany. There will be no shooting unless Germany continues to seek it.

That is my obvious duty in this crisis. That is the clear right of this sovereign nation. This is the only step possible, if we would keep tight the wall of defense which we are pledged to maintain around this Western Hemisphere.

I have no illusions about the gravity of this step. I have not taken it hurriedly or lightly. It is the result of months and months of constant thought and anxiety and prayer. In the protection of your nation and mine it cannot be avoided.

The American people have faced other grave crises in their history—with American courage, with American resolution. They will do no less today.

They know the actualities of the attacks upon us. They know the necessities of a bold defense against these attacks. They know that the times call for clear heads and fearless hearts.

And with that inner strength that comes to a free people conscious of their duty, conscious of the righteousness of what they do, they will—with Divine help and guidance—stand their ground against this latest assault upon their democracy, their sovereignty, and their freedom.

War Message to Congress
Washington, D.C., December 8, 1941

Roosevelt received news of the Japanese attack on Pearl Harbor at 1:50 P.M. on Sunday, December 7, 1941, while lunching at the White House with political advisor, Harry Hopkins. It came in the form of a telephone call from the Secretary of the Navy, Frank Knox. Within a few hours the dimensions of the disaster were clear: 2,403 killed, over 1,000 more wounded, nineteen ships damaged or sunk, almost 200 airplanes destroyed— mostly on the ground. Although a great deal of Japanese military activity had been monitored in the weeks leading up to Pearl Harbor—codes had been broken and messages intercepted—American military commanders on the scene had obviously been caught by surprise as the attacking Japanese task force had penetrated undetected to within a few hundred miles of Honolulu.

The diplomatic background to the attack centered on the oil embargo then in force by America against Japan in retaliation for Japanese aggression in Indochina. The oil embargo was part of a total suspension of trade between America and Japan, and the freezing of Japanese economic assets in America which had been enforced earlier in the year. Diplomatic talks to ease the tensions between America and Japan were ongoing at the time of Pearl Harbor, but were not in a productive mode at the decisive moment. While the diplomats were talking, the Japanese military was considering many factors which spurred them to attack when they did. Weather patterns seemed to give the Japanese the choice of attacking in December or waiting until spring. In December, 1941, they still had oil, enough for another year and a half of war, and they knew that months later their oil situation would probably be worse. An American naval buildup authorized by Congress after the fall of France in June, 1940 had not yet produced much effect, and in December, 1941, the Japanese fleet still dominated the Pacific. The Japanese naval commanders knew that a year or so later, that might no longer be true.

After receiving news of the attack on Pearl Harbor, FDR spoke on the telephone with Winston Churchill, and then met with his cabinet and Vice-President Henry Wallace in the same room of the White House where Lincoln had met with his cabinet when the Civil War began. FDR decided to deliver a concise War Message to Congress the following day, and drafted the seven-minute speech himself with some suggestions from Hopkins. The compelling phrase, "a date which will live in infamy," was an afterthought, penciled in by Roosevelt just before he spoke on December 8th. Although isolationists would still complain about his handling of events, the Pearl Harbor speech to a packed joint session of Congress was punctuated by great applause; and the Congress which had kept Woodrow Wilson hanging for a week in 1917 took only thirty-three minutes to pass the resolution declaring war on Japan in 1941. The vote was 88–0 in the Senate and 388–1 in the House, the only negative vote coming from Jeannette Rankin, Republican of Montana who—as a pacifist— had also voted against war in 1917. On December 11th, Germany and Italy as Japan's allies, declared war on America, and Congress promptly reciprocated. The long and bitter debate over isolationism and America's role on the world stage had finally been overtaken by events.

Mr. Vice President, Mr. Speaker, members of the Senate and the House of Representatives:

Yesterday, December 7, 1941—a date which will live in infamy—the United States of America was suddenly and deliberately attacked by naval and air forces of the empire of Japan.

The United States was at peace with that nation, and, at the solicitation of Japan, was still in conversation with its government and its Emperor looking toward the maintenance of peace in the Pacific.

Indeed, one hour after Japanese air squadrons had commenced bombing in the American island of Oahu, the Japanese Ambassador to the United States and his colleague delivered to our Secretary of State a formal reply to a recent American message. And, while this reply stated that it seemed useless to continue the existing diplomatic negotiations, it contained no threat or hint of war or of armed attack.

It will be recorded that the distance of Hawaii from Japan makes it obvious that the attack was deliberately planned many days or even weeks ago. During the intervening time the Japanese Government has deliberately sought to deceive the United States by false statements and expressions of hope for continued peace.

The attack yesterday on the Hawaiian Islands has caused severe damage to American naval and military forces. I regret to tell you that very many American lives have been lost. In addition, American ships have been reported torpedoed on the high seas between San Francisco and Honolulu.

Yesterday the Japanese Government also launched an attack against Malaya.

Last night Japanese forces attacked Hong Kong.

Last night Japanese forces attacked Guam.

Last night Japanese forces attacked the Philippine Islands.

Last night Japanese forces attacked Wake Island.

And this morning the Japanese attacked Midway Island.

Japan has therefore undertaken a surprise offensive extending through the Pacific Area. The facts of yesterday and today speak for themselves. The people of the United States have already formed their opinions and well understand the implications to the very life and safety of our nation.

As Commander in Chief of the Army and Navy I have directed that all measures be taken for our defense, that always will our whole nation remember the character of the onslaught against us.

No matter how long it may take us to overcome this premeditated invasion, the American people, in their righteous might, will win through absolute victory.

I believe that I interpret the will of the Congress and of the people when I assert that we will not only defend ourselves to the uttermost but will make it very certain that this form of treachery shall never again endanger us.

Hostilities exist. There is no blinking at the fact that our people, our territory and our interests are in grave danger.

With confidence in our armed forces, with the unbounding determination of our people, we will gain the inevitable triumph. So help us God.

I ask that the Congress declare that since the unprovoked and dastardly attack by Japan on Sunday, December 7, 1941, a state of war has existed between the United States and the Japanese Empire.

Fireside Chat
Washington, D.C., February 23, 1942

Roosevelt and many others in his administration were totally aware on December 7, 1941 that the war news they would have to share with their fellow Americans would, for a long time to come, be more bad than good. America was unprepared for war, especially unprepared to strike back soon in any meaningful way against the Japanese in the Pacific. But Roosevelt and his associates also fervently believed that the day would come when the news would be better. The population, natural resources, and industrial strength of America made that inevitable. And it was not their thinking alone. The great Japanese admiral Isoroku Yamamoto also knew that Pearl Harbor was in fact the beginning of the end of Japan's rampantly successful aggression in the Pacific. He knew it would take the United States some time to strike back, but he also feared that Japan would not be able to withstand that strike when it came. His fears were justified.

FDR's Fireside Chat on February 23, 1942 came two and one-half months after Pearl Harbor, when the outlook in the Pacific was bleak. Even the morale-boosting but strategically insignificant bombing attack on Tokyo by Jimmy Doolittle and his men—which would finally give the nation something to cheer about—was still a couple of months in the future. And the immediate headlines on the day of this radio address concerned the imminent fall of the Philippines and the forced retreat from there of General Douglas MacArthur. It wasn't even suspected on this date that General Jonathan Wainwright and his men would be able to hold Corregidor—the last outpost of resistance to the Japanese invasion of the Philippines—as long as they did, finally surrendering on May 6th. FDR put as positive a spin as he could on the situation, and looking back to Tom Paine, Valley Forge and another bleak winter, as was surely appropriate on Washington's Birthday, provided a resounding rallying cry for the war effort then under way.

My Fellow Americans:

Washington's Birthday is a most appropriate occasion for us to talk with each other about things as they are today and things as we know they shall be in the future. For eight years, General Washington and his Continental Army were faced continually with formidable odds and recurring defeats. Supplies and equipment were lacking. In a sense, every winter was a Valley Forge. Throughout the thirteen states there existed fifth columnists—and selfish men, jealous men, fearful men, who proclaimed that Washington's cause was hopeless, and that he should ask for a negotiated peace.

Washington's conduct in those hard times has provided the model for all Americans ever since—a model of moral stamina. He held to his course, as it had been charted in the Declaration of Independence. He and the brave men who served with him knew that no man's life or fortune was secure without freedom and free institutions.

The present great struggle has taught us increasingly that freedom of person and security of property anywhere in the world depend upon the security of the rights and obligations of liberty and justice everywhere in the world.

This war is a new kind of war. It is different from all other wars of the past, not only in its methods and weapons but also in its geography. It is warfare in terms of every continent, every island, every sea, every airlane in the world.

That is the reason why I have asked you to take out and spread before you a map of the whole earth, and to follow with me in the references which I shall make to the world-encircling battle lines of this war. Many questions will, I fear, remain unanswered tonight, but I know you will realize that I cannot cover everything in any one short report to the people. The broad oceans which have been heralded in the past as our protection from attack have become endless battlefields on which we are constantly being challenged by our enemies.

We must all understand and face the hard fact that our job now is to fight at distances which extend all the way around the globe.

We fight at these vast distances because that is where our enemies are. Until our flow of supplies gives us clear superiority we must keep on striking our enemies wherever and whenever we can meet them, even if, for a while, we have to yield ground. Actually, though, we are taking a heavy toll of the enemy every day that goes by.

We must fight at these vast distances to protect our supply lines and our lines of communication with our allies—protect these lines from the enemies who are bending every ounce of their strength, striving against time, to cut them. The object of the Nazis and the Japanese is to of course separate the United States, Britain, China and Russia, and to isolate them one from another, so that each will be surrounded and cut off from sources of supplies and reinforcements. It is the old familiar Axis policy of "divide and conquer."

There are those who still think, however, in terms of the days of sailing-ships. They advise us to pull our warships and our planes and our merchant ships into our own home waters and concentrate solely on last ditch defense. But let me illustrate what would happen if we followed such foolish advice.

Look at your map. Look at the vast area of China, with its millions of fighting men. Look at the vast area of Russia, with its powerful armies and proven military might. Look at the British Isles, Australia, New Zealand, the Dutch Indies, India, the Near East and the Continent of Africa, with their sources of raw materials—their resources of raw materials, and of peoples determined to resist Axis domination. Look too at North America, Central America and South America. It is obvious what would happen if all of these great reservoirs of power were cut off from each other either by enemy action or by self-imposed isolation:

(1.) First, in such a case, we could no longer send aid of any kind to China—to the brave people who, for nearly five years, have withstood Japanese assault, destroyed hundreds of thousands of Japanese soldiers and vast quantities of Japanese war munitions. It is essential that we help China in her magnificent defense and in her inevitable counteroffensive—for that is one important element in the ultimate defeat of Japan.

(2.) Secondly, if we lost communication with the southwest Pacific, all of that area, including Australia and New Zealand and the Dutch Indies, would fall under Japanese domination. Japan in such a case could release great numbers of ships and men to launch attacks on a large scale against the coasts of the Western Hemisphere—South America and Central America, and North America—including Alaska. At the same time, she could immediately extend her conquests in the other direction toward India, through the Indian Ocean, to Africa, to the Near East and try to join forces with Germany and Italy.

(3.) Third, if we were to stop sending munitions to the British and the Russians in the Mediterranean area, in the Persian Gulf and the Red Sea, we would be helping the Nazis to overrun Turkey, and Syria, and Iraq, and Persia—that is now called Iran—Egypt and the Suez Canal, the whole coast of North Africa itself and with that inevitably the whole coast of West Africa—putting Germany within easy striking distance of South America—fifteen hundred miles away.

(4.) Fourth, if by such a fatuous policy, we ceased to protect the North Atlantic supply line to Britain and to Russia, we would help to cripple the splendid counter-offensive by Russia against the Nazis, and we would help to deprive Britain of essential food supplies and munitions.

Those Americans who believed that we could live under the illusion of isolationism wanted the American eagle to imitate the tactics of the ostrich. Now, many of those same people, afraid that we may be sticking our necks out, want our national bird to be turned into a turtle. But we prefer to retain the eagle as it is—flying high and striking hard.

I know I speak for the mass of the American people when I say that we reject the turtle policy and will continue increasingly the policy of carrying the war to the enemy in distant lands and distant waters—as far away as possible from our own home grounds.

There are four main lines of communication now being travelled by our ships: the North Atlantic, the South Atlantic, the Indian Ocean and the South Pacific. These routes are not one-way streets, for the ships that carry our troops and munitions out-bound bring back essential raw materials which we require for our own use.

The maintenance of these vital lines is a very tough job. It is a job which requires tremendous daring, tremendous resourcefulness, and, above all, tremendous production of planes and tanks and guns and also of the ships to carry them. And I speak again for the American people when I say that we can and will do that job.

The defense of the world-wide lines of communication demands— compels relatively safe use by us of the sea and of the air along the various routes; and this, in turn, depends upon control by the United Nations of the many strategic bases along those routes.

Control of the air involves the simultaneous use of two types of planes—first, the long-range heavy bomber; and, second, the light bombers, the dive bombers, the torpedo planes, the short-range pursuit planes, all of which are essential to cooperate with and protect the bases and the bombers themselves.

Heavy bombers can fly under their own power from here to the southwest Pacific, either way, but the smaller planes cannot. Therefore, these lighter planes have to be packed in crates and sent on board cargo ships. Look at your map again; and you will see that the route is long— and at many places perilous—either across the South Atlantic all the way around South Africa and the Cape of Good Hope, or from California to the East Indies direct. A vessel can make a round trip by either route in about four months, or only three round trips in a whole year.

In spite of the length, in spite of the difficulties of this transportation, I can tell you that in two and a half months we already have a large number of bombers and pursuit planes, manned by American pilots and crews, which are now in daily contact with the enemy in the

Southwest Pacific. And thousands of American troops are today in that area engaged in operations not only in the air but on the ground as well.

In this battle area, Japan has had an obvious initial advantage. For she could fly even her short-range planes to the points of attack by using many stepping stones open to her—bases in a multitude of Pacific islands and also bases on the China coast, Indo-China coast, and in Thailand and Malaya. Japanese troop transports could go south from Japan and from China through the narrow China Sea, which can be protected by Japanese planes throughout its whole length.

I ask you to look at your maps again, particularly at that portion of the Pacific Ocean lying west of Hawaii. Before this war even started, the Philippine Islands were already surrounded on three sides by Japanese power. On the west, the China side, the Japanese were in possession of the coast of China and the coast of Indo-China which had been yielded to them by the Vichy French. On the North are the islands of Japan themselves, reaching down almost to northern Luzon. On the east, are the Mandated Islands—which Japan had occupied exclusively, and had fortified in absolute violation of her written word.

The islands that lie between Hawaii and the Philippines—these islands, hundreds of them, appear only as small dots on most maps, or do not appear at all. But they cover a large strategic area. Guam lies in the middle of them—a lone outpost which we have never fortified.

Under the Washington Treaty of 1921 we had solemnly agreed not to add to the fortification of the Philippines. We had no safe naval bases there, so we could not use the islands for extensive naval operations.

Immediately after this war started, the Japanese forces moved down on either side of the Philippines to numerous points south of them—thereby completely encircling the Philippines from north, and south, and east and west.

It is that complete encirclement, with control of the air by Japanese land-based aircraft, which has prevented us from sending substantial reinforcements of men and material to the gallant defenders of the Philippines. For forty years it has always been our strategy—a strategy born of necessity—that in the event of a full-scale attack on the Islands by Japan, we should fight a delaying action, attempting to retire slowly into Bataan Peninsula and Corregidor.

We knew that the war as a whole would have to be fought and won by a process of attrition against Japan itself. We knew all along that, with our greater resources, we could ultimately out-build Japan and ultimately overwhelm her on sea, and on land and in the air. We knew that, to obtain our objective, many varieties of operations would be necessary in areas other than the Philippines.

Now nothing that has occurred in the past two months has caused us to revise this basic strategy of necessity—except that the defense put up by General MacArthur has magnificently exceeded the previous estimates of endurance, and he and his men are gaining eternal glory therefore.

MacArthur's army of Filipinos and Americans, and the forces of the United Nations in China, in Burma and the Netherlands East Indies, are all together fulfilling the same essential task. They are making Japan pay an increasingly terrible price for her ambitious attempts to seize control of the whole Asiatic world. Every Japanese transport sunk off Java is one less transport that they can use to carry reinforcements to their army opposing General MacArthur in Luzon.

It has been said that Japanese gains in the Philippines were made possible only by the success of their surprise attack on Pearl Harbor. I tell you that this is not so.

Even if the attack had not been made your map will show that it would have been a hopeless operation for us to send the Fleet to the Philippines through thousands of miles of ocean, while all those island bases were under the sole control of the Japanese.

The consequences of the attack on Pearl Harbor—serious as they were—have been wildly exaggerated in other ways. And these exaggerations come originally from Axis propagandists; but they have been repeated, I regret to say, by Americans in and out of public life.

You and I have the utmost contempt for Americans who, since Pearl Harbor, have whispered or announced "off the record" that there was no longer any Pacific Fleet—that the Fleet was all sunk or destroyed on December 7th—that more than a thousand of our planes were destroyed on the ground. They have suggested slyly that the Government has withheld the truth about casualties—that eleven or twelve thousand men were killed at Pearl Harbor instead of the figures as officially announced. They have even served the enemy propagandists by spreading the incredible story that ship-loads of bodies of our honored American dead were about to arrive in New York harbor to be put into a common grave.

Almost every Axis broadcast—Berlin, Rome, Tokyo—directly quotes Americans who, by speech or in the press, make damnable misstatements such as these.

The American people realize that in many cases details of military operations cannot be disclosed until we are absolutely certain that the announcement will not give to the enemy military information which he does not already possess.

Your Government has unmistakable confidence in your ability to hear the worst, without flinching or losing heart. You must, in turn, have complete confidence that your Government is keeping nothing from you except information that will help the enemy in his attempt to destroy us. In a democracy there is always a solemn pact of truth between government and the people, but there must also always be a full use of discretion, and that word "discretion" applies to the critics of government as well.

This is war. The American people want to know, and will be told, the general trend of how the war is going. But they do not wish to help the enemy any more than our fighting forces do, and they will pay little attention to the rumor-mongers and the poison peddlers in our midst.

To pass from the realm of rumor and poison to the field of facts: the number of our officers and men killed in the attack on Pearl Harbor on December seventh was 2,340, and the number wounded was 940. Of all of the combatant ships based on Pearl Harbor—battleships, heavy cruisers, light cruisers, aircraft carriers, destroyers and submarines—only three were permanently put out of commission.

Very many of the ships of the Pacific Fleet were not even in Pearl Harbor. Some of those that were there were hit very slightly, and others that were damaged have either rejoined the Fleet by now or are still undergoing repairs. And when those repairs are completed, the ships will be more efficient fighting machines than they were before.

The report that we lost more than a thousand planes at Pearl Harbor is as baseless as the other weird rumors. The Japanese do not know just how many planes they destroyed that day, and I am not going to tell them. But I can say that to date—and including Pearl Harbor—we have destroyed considerably more Japanese planes than they have destroyed of ours.

We have most certainly suffered losses—from Hitler's U-Boats in the Atlantic as well as from the Japanese in the Pacific—and we shall suffer more of them before the turn of the tide. But, speaking for the United States of America, let me say once and for all to the people of the world: We Americans have been compelled to yield ground, but we will regain it. We and the other United Nations are committed to the destruction of the militarism of Japan and Germany. We are daily increasing our strength. Soon, we and not our enemies, will have the offensive; we, not they, will win the final battles; and we, not they, will make the final peace.

Conquered nations in Europe know what the yoke of the Nazis is like. And the people of Korea and of Manchuria know in their flesh the harsh despotism of Japan. All of the people of Asia know that if there is to be an honorable and decent future for any of them or any of us, that future depends on victory by the United Nations over the forces of Axis enslavement.

If a just and durable peace is to be attained, or even if all of us are merely to save our own skins, there is one thought for us here at home to keep uppermost—the fulfillment of our special task of production—uninterrupted production. I stress that word "uninterrupted."

Germany, Italy and Japan are very close to their maximum output of planes, guns, tanks and ships. The United Nations are not—especially the United States of America.

Our first job then is to build up production—uninterrupted production—so that the United Nations can maintain control of the seas and attain control of the air—not merely a slight superiority, but an overwhelming superiority.

On January 6th of this year, I set certain definite goals of production for airplanes, tanks, guns and ships. The Axis propagandists called them fantastic. Tonight, nearly two months later, and after a careful survey of progress by Donald Nelson and others charged with responsibility for our production, I can tell you that those goals will be attained.

In every part of the country, experts in production and the men and women at work in the plants are giving loyal service. With few exceptions, labor, capital and farming realize that this is no time either to make undue profits or to gain special advantages, one over the other.

We are calling for new plants and additions—additions to old plants. We are calling for plant conversion to war needs. We are seeking more men and more women to run them. We are working longer hours. We are coming to realize that one extra plane or extra tank or extra gun or extra ship completed tomorrow may, in a few months, turn the tide on some distant battlefield; it may make the difference between life and death for some of our own fighting men. We know now that if we lose this war it will be generations or even centuries before our conception of democracy can live again. And we can lose this war only if we slow up our effort or if we waste our ammunition sniping at each other.

Here are three high purposes for every American:

(1.) We shall not stop work for a single day. If any dispute arises we shall keep on working while the dispute is solved by mediation, or conciliation or arbitration—until the war is won.

(2.) We shall not demand special gains or special privileges or special advantages for any one group or occupation.

(3.) We shall give up conveniences and modify the routine of our lives if our country asks us to do so. We will do it cheerfully, remembering that the common enemy seeks to destroy every home and every freedom in every part of our land.

This generation of Americans has come to realize, with a present and personal realization, that there is something larger and more

important than the life of any individual or of any individual group—
something for which a man will sacrifice, and gladly sacrifice, not only
his pleasures, not only his goods, not only his associations with those he
loves, but his life itself. In time of crisis when the future is in the balance, we come to understand, with full recognition and devotion, what
this nation is and what we owe to it.

The Axis propagandists have tried in various evil ways to destroy our
determination and our morale. Failing in that, they are now trying to
destroy our confidence in our own allies. They say that the British are
finished—that the Russians and the Chinese are about to quit. Patriotic
and sensible Americans will reject these absurdities. And instead of listening to any of this crude propaganda, they will recall some of the
things that Nazis and Japanese have said and are still saying about us.
Ever since this nation became the arsenal of democracy—ever since
enactment of Lend-Lease—there has been one persistent theme
through all Axis propaganda.

This theme has been that Americans are admittedly rich, that
Americans have considerable industrial power—but that Americans
are soft and decadent, that they cannot and will not unite and work and
fight.

From Berlin, Rome and Tokyo we have been described as a nation
of weaklings—"playboys"—who would hire British soldiers, or Russian
soldiers, or Chinese soldiers to do our fighting for us.

Let them repeat that now! Let them tell that to General MacArthur
and his men. Let them tell that to the sailors who today are hitting hard
in the far waters of the Pacific. Let them tell that to the boys in the
Flying Fortresses. Let them tell that to the Marines!

The United Nations constitute an association of independent
peoples of equal dignity and equal importance. The United Nations are
dedicated to a common cause. We share equally and with equal zeal
the anguish and the awful sacrifices of war. In the partnership of our
common enterprise, we must share in a unified plan in which all of us
must play our several parts, each of us being equally indispensable and
dependent one on the other.

We have unified command and cooperation and comradeship.

We Americans will contribute unified production and unified acceptance of sacrifice and of effort. That means a national unity that can
know no limitations of race or creed or selfish politics. The American
people expect that much from themselves. And the American people
will find ways and means of expressing their determination to their enemies, including the Japanese Admiral who has said that he will dictate
the terms of peace here in the White House.

We of the United Nations are agreed on certain broad principles in the kind of peace we seek. The Atlantic Charter applies not only to the parts of the world that border the Atlantic but to the whole world; disarmament of aggressors, self-determination of nations and peoples, and the four freedoms—freedom of speech, freedom of religion, freedom from want, and freedom from fear.

The British and the Russian people have known the full fury of Nazi onslaught. There have been times when the fate of London and Moscow was in serious doubt. But there was never the slightest question that either the British or the Russians would yield. And today all the United Nations salute the superb Russian Army as it celebrates the twenty-fourth anniversary of its first assembly.

Though their homeland was overrun, the Dutch people are still fighting stubbornly and powerfully overseas.

The great Chinese people have suffered grievous losses; Chungking has been almost wiped out of existence—yet it remains the capital of an unbeatable China.

That is the conquering spirit which prevails throughout the United Nations in this war.

The task that we Americans now face will test us to the uttermost. Never before have we been called upon for such a prodigious effort. Never before have we had so little time in which to do so much.

"These are the times that try men's souls."

Tom Paine wrote those words on a drumhead, by the light of a campfire. That was when Washington's little army of ragged, rugged men was retreating across New Jersey, having tasted naught but defeat.

And General Washington ordered that these great words written by Tom Paine be read to the men of every regiment in the Continental Army, and this was the assurance given to the first American armed forces:

"The summer soldier and the sunshine patriot will, in this crisis, shrink from the service of their country; but he that stands it now, deserves the love and thanks of man and woman. Tyranny, like hell, is not easily conquered, yet we have this consolation with us, that the harder the sacrifice, the more glorious the triumph."

So spoke Americans in the year 1776. So speak Americans today!

Fireside Chat
Washington, D.C., October 12, 1942

Roosevelt did several radio broadcasts during World War II to give what he hoped would be inspirational progress reports on the home front, this one following a tour of war production plants and military training bases. The task of organizing the war effort on the home front was an immense undertaking, and many new federal agencies were created—with FDR the final arbiter of disputes among them, and between them and the military—to allocate resources and manpower, control prices and spending, establish priorities and set goals. By the start of 1944, from very modest beginnings, American war production was double that of the Axis powers combined. By the end of the conflict, American industry had met goals which would have seemed inconceivable before 1941, turning out 6,500 naval vessels, almost 300,000 airplanes, over 80,000 tanks, and providing the equipment for 15 million men and women in uniform. More than $2 billion of the war effort went into the Manhattan Project's development of the atomic bomb. It was first tested on July 6, 1945, and then used by President Truman to bring an end to the war with Japan a few weeks later. The war touched almost everyone. Thirty-one million men were registered with the Selective Service, and about half of them actually served in the military. More than 6 million Americans moved from rural areas to jobs in war plants and factories. This speech by FDR about progress on the home front was given a month before the November, 1942 invasion of North Africa, the crucial first step in turning the tide of World War II in Europe.

My Fellow Americans:

As you know, I have recently come back from a trip of inspection of camps and training stations and war factories.

The main thing that I observed on this trip is not exactly news. It is the plain fact that the American people are united as never before in their determination to do a job and to do it well.

This whole nation of one hundred and thirty million free men, women and children is becoming one great fighting force. Some of us are soldiers or sailors, some of us are civilians. Some of us are fighting the war in airplanes five miles above the continent of Europe or the islands of the Pacific—and some of us are fighting it in mines deep down in the earth of Pennsylvania or Montana. A few of us are decorated with medals for heroic achievement, but all of us can have that deep and permanent inner satisfaction that comes from doing the best we know how—each of us playing an honorable part in the great struggle to save our democratic civilization.

Whatever our individual circumstances or opportunities—we are all in it, and our spirit is good, and we Americans and our allies are going to win—and do not let anyone tell you anything different.

That is the main thing that I saw on my trip around the country—unbeatable spirit. If the leaders of Germany and Japan could have come along with me, and had seen what I saw, they would agree with my conclusions. Unfortunately, they were unable to make the trip with me. And that is one reason why we are carrying our war effort overseas—to them.

With every passing week the war increases in scope and intensity. That is true in Europe, in Africa, in Asia, and on all the seas.

The strength of the United Nations is on the upgrade in this war. The Axis leaders, on the other hand, know by now that they have already reached their full strength, and that their steadily mounting losses in men and material cannot be fully replaced. Germany and Japan are already realizing what the inevitable result will be when the total strength of the United Nations hits them—at additional places on the earth's surface.

One of the principal weapons of our enemies in the past has been their use of what is called "The War of Nerves." They have spread falsehood and terror; they have started Fifth Columns everywhere; they have duped the innocent; they have fomented suspicion and hate between neighbors; they have aided and abetted those people in other nations—including our own—whose words and deeds are advertised from Berlin and from Tokyo as proof of our disunity.

The greatest defense against all such propaganda, of course, is the common sense of the common people—and that defense is prevailing.

The "War of Nerves" against the United Nations is now turning into a boomerang. For the first time, the Nazi propaganda machine is on the defensive. They begin to apologize to their own people for the repulse of their vast forces at Stalingrad, and for the enormous casualties they are suffering. They are compelled to beg their overworked people to rally their weakened production. They even publicly admit, for the first time, that Germany can be fed only at the cost of stealing food from the rest of Europe.

They are proclaiming that a second front is impossible; but, at the same time, they are desperately rushing troops in all directions, and stringing barbed wire all the way from the coasts of Finland and Norway to the islands of the Eastern Mediterranean. Meanwhile, they are driven to increase the fury of their atrocities.

The United Nations have decided to establish the identity of those Nazi leaders who are responsible for the innumerable acts of savagery. As each of these criminal deeds is committed, it is being carefully investigated; and the evidence is being relentlessly piled up for the future purposes of justice.

We have made it entirely clear that the United Nations seek no mass reprisals against the populations of Germany or Italy or Japan. But the ring leaders and their brutal henchmen must be named, and apprehended, and tried in accordance with the judicial processes of criminal law.

There are now millions of Americans in army camps, in naval stations, in factories and in shipyards.

Who are these millions upon whom the life of our country depends? What are they thinking? What are their doubts? What are their hopes? And how is the work progressing?

The Commander-in-Chief cannot learn all of the answers to these questions in Washington. And that is why I made the trip I did.

It is very easy to say, as some have said, that when the President travels through the country he should go with a blare of trumpets, with crowds on the sidewalks, with batteries of reporters and photographers—talking and posing with all of the politicians of the land.

But having had some experience in this war and in the last war, I can tell you very simply that the kind of trip I took permitted me to concentrate on the work I had to do without expending time, meeting all the demands of publicity. And—I might add—it was a particular pleasure to make a tour of the country without having to give a single thought to politics.

I expect to make other trips for similar purposes, and I shall make them in the same way.

In the last war, I had seen great factories; but until I saw some of the new present-day plants, I had not thoroughly visualized our American war effort. Of course, I saw only a small portion of all our plants, but that portion was a good cross-section, and it was deeply impressive.

The United States has been at war for only ten months, and is engaged in the enormous talk of multiplying its armed forces many times. We are by no means at full production level yet. But I could not help asking myself on the trip, where would we be today if the Government of the United States had not begun to build many of its factories for this huge increase more than two years ago, more than a year before war was forced upon us at Pearl Harbor?

We have also had to face the problem of shipping. Ships in every part of the world continue to be sunk by enemy action. But the total tonnage of ships coming out of American, Canadian and British shipyards, day by day, has increased so fast that we are getting ahead of our enemies in the bitter battle of transportation.

In expanding our shipping, we have had to enlist many thousands of men for our Merchant Marine. These men are serving magnificently. They are risking their lives every hour so that guns and tanks and planes and ammunition and food may be carried to the heroic defenders of Stalingrad and to all the United Nations' forces all over the world.

A few days ago I awarded the first Maritime Distinguished Service Medal to a young man—Edward F. Cheney of Yeadon, Pennsylvania— who had shown great gallantry in rescuing his comrades from the oily waters of the sea after their ship had been torpedoed. There will be many more such acts of bravery. In one sense my recent trip was a hurried one, out through the Middle West, to the Northwest, down the length of the Pacific Coast and back through the Southwest and the South. In another sense, however, it was a leisurely trip, because I had the opportunity to talk to the people who are actually doing the work— management and labor alike—on their own home grounds. And it gave me a fine chance to do some thinking about the major problems of our war effort on the basis of first things first.

As I told the three press association representatives who accompanied me, I was impressed by the large proportion of women employed—doing skilled manual labor running machines. As time goes on, and many more of our men enter the armed forces, this proportion of women will increase. Within less than a year from now, I think, there will probably be as many women as men working in our war production plants.

I had some enlightening experiences relating to the old saying of us men that curiosity—inquisitiveness—is stronger among women. I noticed, frequently, that when we drove unannounced down the middle aisle of a great plant full of workers and machines, the first people to look up from their work were the men—and not the women. It was chiefly the men who were arguing as to whether that fellow in the straw hat was really the President or not.

So having seen the quality of the work and of the workers on our production lines—and coupling these firsthand observations with the reports of actual performance of our weapons on the fighting fronts—I can say to you that we are getting ahead of our enemies in the battle of production.

And of great importance to our future production was the effective and rapid manner in which the Congress met the serious problem of the rising cost of living. It was a splendid example of the operation of democratic processes in wartime.

The machinery to carry out this act of the Congress was put into effect within twelve hours after the bill was signed. The legislation will help the cost-of-living problems of every worker in every factory and on every farm in the land.

In order to keep stepping up our production, we have had to add millions of workers to the total labor force of the Nation. And as new factories came into operation, we must find additional millions of workers.

This presents a formidable problem in the mobilization of manpower.

It is not that we do not have enough people in this country to do the job. The problem is to have the right numbers of the right people in the right places at the right time.

We are learning to ration materials, and we must now learn to ration manpower. The major objectives of a sound manpower policy are:

First, to select and train men of the highest fighting efficiency needed for our armed forces in the achievement of victory over our enemies in combat.

Second, to man our war industries and farms with the workers needed to produce the arms and munitions and food required by ourselves and by our fighting allies to win this war.

In order to do this, we shall be compelled to stop workers from moving from one war job to another as a matter of personal preference; to stop employers from stealing labor from each other; to use older men, and handicapped people, and more women, and even grown boys and girls, wherever possible and reasonable, to replace men of military age and fitness; to train new personnel for essential war work; and to stop the wastage of labor in all non-essential activities.

There are many other things that we can do, and do immediately, to help meet this manpower problem.

The school authorities in all the states should work out plans to enable our high school students to take some time from their school year, to use their summer vacations, to help farmers raise and harvest their crops, or to work somewhere in the war industries. This does not mean closing schools and stopping education. It does mean giving older students a better opportunity to contribute their bit to the war effort. Such work will do no harm to the students.

People should do their work as near their homes as possible. We cannot afford to transport a single worker into an area where there is already a worker available to do the job.

In some communities, employers dislike to employ women. In others they are reluctant to hire Negroes. In still others, older men are not wanted. We can no longer afford to indulge such prejudices or practices.

Every citizen wants to know what essential war work he can do the best. He can get the answer by applying to the nearest United States Employment Service office. There are four thousand five hundred of these offices throughout the Nation. They form the corner grocery stores of our manpower system. This network of employment offices is prepared to advise every citizen where his skills and labors are needed most, and to refer him to an employer who can utilize them to best advantage in the war effort.

Perhaps the most difficult phase of the manpower problem is the scarcity of farm labor in many places. I have seen evidences of the fact, however, that the people are trying to meet it as well as possible.

In one community that I visited a perishable crop was harvested by turning out the whole of the high school for three or four days.

And in another community of fruit growers the usual Japanese labor was not available; but when the fruit ripened, the banker, the butcher, the lawyer, the garage man, the druggist, the local editor, and in fact every able-bodied man and woman in the town, left their occupations, went out gathering the fruit, and sent it to market.

Every farmer in the land must realize fully that his production is part of war production, and that he is regarded by the Nation as essential to victory. The American people expect him to keep his production up, and even to increase it. We will use every effort to help him to get labor; but, at the same time, he and the people of his community must use ingenuity and cooperative effort to produce crops, and livestock and dairy products.

It may be that all of our volunteer effort—however well intentioned and well administered—will not suffice wholly to solve this problem. In that case, we shall have to adopt new legislation. And if this is necessary, I do not believe that the American people will shrink from it.

In a sense, every American, because of the privilege of his citizenship, is a part of the Selective Service.

The Nation owes a debt of gratitude to the Selective Service Boards. The successful operation of the Selective Service System and the way it has been accepted by the great mass of our citizens give us confidence that if necessary, the same principle could be used to solve any manpower problem.

And I want to say also a word of praise and thanks to the more than ten million people, all over the country, who have volunteered for the work of civilian defense—and who are working hard at it. They are displaying unselfish devotion in the patient performance of their often tiresome and always anonymous tasks. In doing this important neighborly work they are helping to fortify our national unity and our real understanding of the fact that we are all involved in this war.

Naturally, on my trip I was most interested in watching the training of our fighting forces.

All of our combat units that go overseas must consist of young, strong men who have had thorough training. An Army division that has an average age of twenty-three or twenty-four is a better fighting unit than one which has an average age of thirty-three or thirty-four. The more of such troops we have in the field, the sooner the war will be won, and the smaller will be the cost in casualties.

Therefore, I believe that it will be necessary to lower the present minimum age limit for Selective Service from twenty years down to eighteen. We have learned how inevitable that is—and how important to the speeding up of victory.

I can very thoroughly understand the feelings of all parents whose sons have entered our armed forces. I have an appreciation of that feeling and so has my wife. I want every father and every mother who has a son in the service to know—again, from what I have seen with my own eyes—that the men in the Army, Navy and Marine Corps are receiving today the best possible training, equipment and medical care. And we will never fail to provide for the spiritual needs of our officers and men under the Chaplains of our armed services.

Good training will save many, many lives in battle. The highest rate of casualties is always suffered by units comprised of inadequately trained men.

We can be sure that the combat units of our Army and Navy are well manned, well equipped, well trained. Their effectiveness in action will depend upon the quality of their leadership, and upon the wisdom of the strategic plans on which all military operations are based.

I can say one thing about these plans of ours: They are not being decided by the typewriter strategists who expound their views in the press or on the radio.

One of the greatest of American soldiers, Robert E. Lee, once remarked on the tragic fact that in the war of his day all of the best generals were apparently working on newspapers instead of in the Army. And that seems to be true in all wars. The trouble with the typewriter strategists is that while they may be full of bright ideas, they are not in possession of much information about the facts or problems of military operations.

We, therefore, will continue to leave the plans for this war to the military leaders. The military and naval plans of the United States are made by the Joint Staff of the Army and Navy which is constantly in session in Washington. The Chiefs of this Staff are Admiral Leahy, General Marshall, Admiral King and General Arnold. They meet and confer regularly with representatives of the British Joint Staff, and with representatives of Russia, China, the Netherlands, Poland, Norway, the British Dominions and other nations working in the common cause.

Since this unity of operations was put into effect last January, there has been a very substantial agreement between these planners, all of whom are trained in the profession of arms—air, sea and land—from their early years. As Commander-in-Chief I have at all times also been in substantial agreement.

As I have said before, many major decisions of strategy have been made. One of them—on which we have all agreed—relates to the necessity of diverting enemy forces from Russia and China to other theaters of war by new offensives against Germany and Japan. An announcement of how these offensives are to be launched, and when, and where, cannot be broadcast over the radio at this time.

We are celebrating today the exploit of a bold and adventurous Italian—Christopher Columbus—who with the aid of Spain opened up a new world where freedom and tolerance and respect for human rights and dignity provided an asylum for the oppressed of the old world.

Today, the sons of the New World are fighting in lands far distant from their own America. They are fighting to save for all mankind, including ourselves, the principles which have flourished in this new world of freedom.

We are mindful of the countless millions of people whose future liberty and whose very lives depend upon permanent victory for the United Nations.

There are a few people in this country who, when the collapse of the Axis begins, will tell our people that we are safe once more; that we can tell the rest of the world to "stew in its own juice"; that never again will we help to pull "the other fellow's chestnuts from the fire"; that the future of civilization can jolly well take care of itself insofar as we are concerned.

But it is useless to win battles if the cause for which we fight these battles is lost. It is useless to win a war unless it stays won.

We, therefore, fight for the restoration and perpetuation of faith and hope and peace throughout the world.

The objective of today is clear and realistic. It is to destroy completely the military power of Germany, Italy and Japan to such good purpose that their threat against us and all the other United Nations cannot be revived a generation hence. We are united in seeking the kind of victory that will guarantee that our grandchildren can grow and, under God may live their lives, free from the constant threat of invasion, destruction, slavery and violent death.

Radio Address to *New York Herald Tribune* Forum
Washington, D.C., November 17, 1942

Some of the gloom following Pearl Harbor had clearly lifted by the time of this radio address from the White House—the final session of a "Forum on Current Problems" sponsored by the *New York Herald Tribune* in November, 1942. In addition to the participants in the Forum assembled at New York's Waldorf-Astoria, a huge radio audience—estimated at over 36 million people—heard FDR commemorate the recent decisive naval victory in the Solomon Islands and the success of the Allies' ongoing North African campaign.

Ladies and gentlemen, I have always welcomed the opportunity to participate in the Herald Tribune Forum because I have always been interested in the public presentation of all kinds of national problems.

In time of peace every variety of problem and issue is an interesting subject for public discussion.

But in time of war the American people know that the one all-important job before them is fighting and working to win. Therefore, of necessity, while long-range social and economic problems are by no means forgotten, they are a little like books which for the moment we have laid aside in order that we might get out the old atlas to learn the geography of the battle areas.

In time of war your government cannot always give spot news to the people. Nearly everybody understands that—and the reason for it.

This means that those relatively few people who do have the facts from all over the world, not only every day but every hour of every day, are somewhat precluded from discussing these facts publicly, except in the most general of terms. If they did, they would almost inevitably say things which would help the people who are trying to destroy us.

In reverse, those who are not in possession of all the news must almost inevitably speak from guesswork based on information of doubtful accuracy. They do not know the facts, and therefore the value of their statements becomes greatly reduced. Nor must we, in the actual progress of the war, lend ears to the clamor of politics or to criticism from those who, as we know in our hearts, are actuated by political motives.

The fact that this type of criticism has done less harm in the United States than might be expected has been due to the good old horse sense of the American people. I know from a somewhat long experience — in war time as well as peace time — that the overwhelming majority of our people know how to discriminate in their reading and in their radio listening between informed discussion and verbal thrusts in the dark.

I think you will realize that I have made a constant effort as Commander-in-Chief to keep politics out of the fighting of this war.

But I must confess that my foot slipped once. About ten days before the late Election Day one of our aircraft carriers was torpedoed in the southwest Pacific. She did not sink at once, but it became clear that she could not make port. She was, therefore, destroyed by our own forces. We in Washington did not know whether the enemy was aware of her sinking — for there were no Japanese ships near enough to see her go down. You will realize, of course, that the actual knowledge of the loss of enemy ships has a definite bearing on continuing naval operations for some time after the event. We, for instance, know that we have sunk a number of Japanese aircraft carriers and we know that we have bombed or torpedoed others. We would give a king's ransom to know whether the latter were sunk, or were saved, repaired and put back into commission.

However, when we got news of the sinking of this particular ship a great issue was being raised in the Congress and in the public vehicles of information as to the suppression of news from the fighting fronts. There was a division of opinion among responsible authorities.

Here came my mistake. I yielded to the clamor. I did so partly in realization of the certainty that if the news of the sinking were given out two or three weeks later it would be publicly charged that the news had been suppressed by me until after the election.

Then, shortly thereafter protests came from the admirals in command in the southwest Pacific and at our great base in Hawaii on the ground that, in all probability, the Japanese Navy had no information of the sinking, and that handing them the information on a silver platter — although we were careful not to reveal the name of the carrier — still gave to the Japanese a military advantage which they would otherwise not have had.

This confession of mine illustrates to the people of this country the fact that in time of war the conduct of that war, with the aim of victory, comes absolutely first. They know that not one of their inalienable rights is taken away through the failure to disclose to them, for a reasonable length of time, facts that Hitler and Mussolini and Tojo would give their eyeteeth to learn. Facts, therefore, become paramount—facts that cannot be told to the public at the time, as well as facts that can and should be told at all times.

The posters that tell you, "Loose talk costs lives," do not exaggerate. Loose talk delays victory. Loose talk is the damp that gets into powder. We prefer to keep our powder dry.

We have a gigantic job to do—all of us, together. Our battle lines today stretch from Kiska to Murmansk, from Tunisia to Guadalcanal. These lines will grow longer, as our forces advance.

Yes, we have had an uphill fight, and it will continue to be uphill, all the way. There can be no coasting to victory.

During the last two weeks we have had a great deal of good news and it would seem that the turning point of this war has at last been reached. But this is no time for exultation. There is no time now for anything but fighting and working to win.

A few days ago, as our Army advanced through North Africa, on the other side of the world our Navy was fighting what was one of the greatest battles of our history.

A very powerful Japanese force was moving at night toward our positions in the Solomon Islands. The spearhead of the force that we sent to intercept the enemy was under the command of Rear Admiral Daniel J. Callaghan. He was aboard the leading ship, the cruiser San Francisco.

The San Francisco sailed right into the enemy fleet—right through the whole enemy fleet—her guns blazing. She engaged and hit three enemy vessels, sinking one of them. At point-blank range she engaged an enemy battleship—heavily her superior in size and firepower. She silenced this battleship's big guns and so disabled her that she could be sunk by torpedoes from our destroyers and aircraft.

The San Francisco herself was hit many times. Admiral Callaghan, my close personal friend, and many of his gallant officers and men gave their lives in this battle. But the San Francisco was brought safely back to port by a lieutenant commander, and she will fight again for her country.

The commander of the task force of which the San Francisco was a part has recommended that she be the first of our Navy's vessels to be decorated for outstanding service.

But there are no citations, no medals, which carry with them such high honor as that accorded to fighting men by the respect of their comrades-in-arms.

The commanding general of the Marines in Guadalcanal, General Vandergrift, yesterday sent a message to the commander of the fleet, Admiral Halsey, saying, "We lift our battered helmets in admiration for those who fought magnificently against overwhelming odds and drove the enemy back to crushing defeat."

Let us thank God for such men as these. May our nation continue to be worthy of them, throughout this war, and forever.

Fireside Chat (on GI Bill of Rights)
Washington, D.C., July 28, 1943

In this Fireside Chat in the summer of 1943—in the immediate aftermath of the collapse of Italian fascism and the resignation of Mussolini on July 25th—FDR outlined the provisions of what would become known as the GI Bill of Rights. These were the benefits the nation could and would extend to the men and women who served in the armed forces once peace came. Peace was still two years away, and everywhere FDR stressed that it must be total victory, unconditional surrender, nothing less was acceptable; but he also felt it wasn't too soon to look ahead. Harkening back to the Depression in which his presidency began, he was able to put his fears and concerns very simply and graphically: "They [the returning soldiers and sailors] must not be demobilized into an environment of inflation and unemployment, to a place on a bread line or on a corner selling apples."

My Fellow Americans:

Over a year and a half ago I said this to the Congress: "The militarists in Berlin, and Rome and Tokyo started this war, but the massed angered forces of common humanity will finish it."

Today that prophecy is in the process of being fulfilled. The massed, angered forces of common humanity are on the march. They are going forward—on the Russian front, in the vast Pacific area, and into Europe—converging upon their ultimate objectives: Berlin and Tokyo.

I think the first crack in the Axis has come. The criminal, corrupt Fascist regime in Italy is going to pieces.

The pirate philosophy of the Fascists and the Nazis cannot stand adversity. The military superiority of the United Nations—on sea and land, and in the air—has been applied in the right place and at the right time.

Hitler refused to send sufficient help to save Mussolini. In fact, Hitler's troops in Sicily stole the Italians' motor equipment, leaving

Italian soldiers so stranded that they had no choice but to surrender. Once again the Germans betrayed their Italian allies, as they had done time and time again on the Russian front and in the long retreat from Egypt, through Libya and Tripoli, to the final surrender in Tunisia.

And so Mussolini came to the reluctant conclusion that the "jig was up"; he could see the shadow of the long arm of justice. But he and his Fascist gang will be brought to book, and punished for their crimes against humanity. No criminal will be allowed to escape by the expedient of "resignation."

So our terms to Italy are still the same as our terms to Germany and Japan—"unconditional surrender."

We will have no truck with Fascism in any way, in any shape or manner. We will permit no vestige of Fascism to remain.

Eventually Italy will reconstitute herself. It will be the people of Italy who will do that, choosing their own government in accordance with the basic democratic principles of liberty and equality. In the meantime, the United Nations will not follow the pattern set by Mussolini and Hitler and the Japanese for the treatment of occupied countries— the pattern of pillage and starvation.

We are already helping the Italian people in Sicily. With their cordial cooperation, we are establishing and maintaining security and order—we are dissolving the organizations which have kept them under Fascist tyranny—we are providing them with the necessities of life until the time comes when they can fully provide for themselves.

Indeed, the people in Sicily today are rejoicing in the fact that for the first time in years they are permitted to enjoy the fruits of their own labor—they can eat what they themselves grow, instead of having it stolen from them by the Fascists and the Nazis.

In every country conquered by the Nazis and the Fascists, or the Japanese militarists, the people have been reduced to the status of slaves or chattels.

It is our determination to restore these conquered peoples to the dignity of human beings, masters of their own fate, entitled to freedom of speech, freedom of religion, freedom from want, and freedom from fear.

We have started to make good on that promise.

I am sorry if I step on the toes of those Americans who, playing party politics at home, call that kind of foreign policy "crazy altruism" and "starry-eyed dreaming."

Meanwhile, the war in Sicily and Italy goes on. It must go on, and will go on, until the Italian people realize the futility of continuing to fight in a lost cause—a cause to which the people of Italy never gave their wholehearted approval and support. It's a little over a year since we planned the North African campaign. It is six months since we planned the Sicilian campaign. I confess that I am of an impatient disposition, but I think that I understand and that most people understand the amount of time necessary to prepare for any major military or naval operation. We cannot just pick up the telephone and order a new campaign to start the next week.

For example, behind the invasion forces in North Africa, the invasion forces that went out of North Africa, were thousands of ships and planes guarding the long, perilous sea lanes, carrying the men, carrying the equipment and the supplies to the point of attack. And behind all these were the railroad lines and the highways here back home that carried the men and the munitions to the ports of embarkation—there were the factories and the mines and the farms here back home that turned out the materials—there were the training camps here back home where the men learned how to perform the strange and difficult and dangerous tasks which were to meet them on the beaches and in the deserts and in the mountains.

All this had to be repeated, first in North Africa and then in Sicily. Here the factor—in Sicily—the factor of air attack was added—for we could use North Africa as the base for softening up the landing places and lines of defense in Sicily, and the lines of supply in Italy.

It is interesting for us to realize that every flying fortress that bombed harbor installations at, for example, Naples, bombed it from its base in North Africa, required 1,110 gallons of gasoline for each single mission, and that this is the equal of about 375 "A" ration tickets—enough gas to drive your car five times across this continent. You will better understand your part in the war—and what gasoline rationing means—if you multiply this by the gasoline needs of thousands of planes and hundreds of thousands of jeeps, and trucks and tanks that are now serving overseas.

I think that the personal convenience of the individual, or the individual family back home here in the United States will appear somewhat less important when I tell you that the initial assault force on Sicily involved 3,000 ships which carried 160,000 men—Americans, British, Canadians and French—together with 14,000 vehicles, 600 tanks, and 1,800 guns. And this initial force was followed every day and every night by thousands of reinforcements.

The meticulous care with which the operation in Sicily was planned has paid dividends. Our casualties in men, in ships and material have been low—in fact, far below our estimate.

And all of us are proud of the superb skill and courage of the officers and men who have conducted and are conducting those operations. The toughest resistance developed on the front of the British Eighth

Army, which included the Canadians. But that is no new experience for that magnificent fighting force which has made the Germans pay a heavy price for each hour of delay in the final victory. The American Seventh Army, after a stormy landing on the exposed beaches of Southern Sicily, swept with record speed across the island into the capital at Palermo. For many of our troops this was their first battle experience, but they have carried themselves like veterans. And we must give credit for the coordination of the diverse forces in the field, and for the planning of the whole campaign, to the wise and skillful leadership of General Eisenhower. Admiral Cunningham, General Alexander and Sir Marshal Tedder have been towers of strength in handling the complex details of naval and ground and air activities.

You have heard some people say that the British and the Americans can never get along well together—you have heard some people say that the Army and the Navy and the Air Forces can never get along well together—that real cooperation between them is impossible. Tunisia and Sicily have given the lie, once and for all, to those narrow-minded prejudices.

The dauntless fighting spirit of the British people in this war has been expressed in the historic words and deeds of Winston Churchill—and the world knows how the American people feel about him.

Ahead of us are much bigger fights. We and our Allies will go into them as we went into Sicily—together. And we shall carry on together.

Today our production of ships is almost unbelievable. This year we are producing over nineteen million tons of merchant shipping and next year our production will be over twenty-one million tons. And in addition to our shipments across the Atlantic, we must realize that in this war we are operating in the Aleutians, in the distant parts of the Southwest Pacific, in India, and off the shores of South America. For several months we have been losing fewer ships by sinkings, and we have been destroying more and more U-boats. We hope this will continue. But we cannot be sure. We must not lower our guard for one single instant.

An example—a tangible result of our great increase in merchant shipping—which I think will be good news to civilians at home—is that tonight we are able to terminate the rationing of coffee. And we also expect that within a short time we shall get greatly increased allowances of sugar.

Those few Americans who grouse and complain about the inconveniences of life here in the United States should learn some lessons from the civilian populations of our Allies—Britain, and China, and Russia—and of all the lands occupied by our common enemies.

The heaviest and most decisive fighting today is going on in Russia.

I am glad that the British and we have been able to contribute somewhat to the great striking power of the Russian armies.

In 1941–1942 the Russians were able to retire without breaking, to move many of their war plants from western Russia far into the interior, to stand together with complete unanimity in the defense of their homeland.

The success of the Russian armies has shown that it is dangerous to make prophecies about them—a fact which has been forcibly brought home to that mystic master of strategic intuition, Herr Hitler.

The short-lived German offensive, launched early this month, was a desperate attempt to bolster the morale of the German people. The Russians were not fooled by this. They went ahead with their own plans for attack—plans which coordinate with the whole United Nations' offensive strategy.

The world has never seen greater devotion, determination and self-sacrifice than have been displayed by the Russian people and their armies, under the leadership of Marshal Joseph Stalin.

With a nation which in saving itself is thereby helping to save all the world from the Nazi menace, this country of ours should always be glad to be a good neighbor and a sincere friend in the world of the future.

In the Pacific, we are pushing the Japs around from the Aleutians to New Guinea. There too we have taken the initiative—and we are not going to let go of it. It becomes clearer and clearer that the attrition, the whittling down process against the Japanese is working. The Japs have lost more planes and more ships than they have been able to replace.

The continuous and energetic prosecution of the war of attrition will drive the Japs back from their over-extended line running from Burma and the Straits Settlement and Siam through the Netherlands Indies to eastern New Guinea and the Solomons. And we have good reason to believe that their shipping and their air power cannot support such outposts.

Our naval and land and air strength in the Pacific is constantly growing. And if the Japanese are basing their future plans for the Pacific on a long period in which they will be permitted to consolidate and exploit their conquered resources, they had better start revising their plans now. I give that to them merely as a helpful suggestion. We are delivering planes and vital war supplies for the heroic armies of Generalissimo Chiang Kai-shek, and we must do more at all costs.

Our air supply line from India to China across enemy territory continues despite attempted Japanese interference. We have seized the initiative from the Japanese in the air over Burma and now we enjoy superiority. We are bombing Japanese communications, supply dumps, and bases in China, in Indo-China, in Burma. But we are still far from our main objectives in the war against Japan. Let us remember, however, how far we were a year ago from any of our objectives in the European theatre. We are pushing forward to occupation of positions which in time will enable us to attack the Japanese Islands themselves from the North, from the South, from the East, and from the West.

You have heard it said that while we are succeeding greatly on the fighting front, we are failing miserably on the home front. I think this is another of those immaturities—a false slogan easy to state but untrue in the essential facts.

For the longer this war goes on the clearer it becomes that no one can draw a blue pencil down the middle of a page and call one side "the fighting front" and the other side "the home front." For the two of them are inexorably tied together.

Every combat division, every naval task force, every squadron of fighting planes is dependent for its equipment and ammunition and fuel and food, as indeed it is for its manpower, dependent on the American people in civilian clothes in the offices and in the factories and on the farms at home.

The same kind of careful planning that gained victory in North Africa and Sicily is required, if we are to make victory an enduring reality and do our share in building the kind of peaceful world that will justify the sacrifices made in this war. The United Nations are substantially agreed on the general objectives for the post-war world. They are also agreed that this is not the time to engage in an international discussion of all the terms of peace and all the details of the future. Let us win the war first. We must not relax our pressure on the enemy by taking time out to define every boundary and settle every political controversy in every part of the world. The important thing—the all-important thing now is to get on with the war—and to win it.

While concentrating on military victory, we are not neglecting the planning of the things to come, the freedoms which we know will make for more decency and greater justice throughout the world.

Among many other things we are, today, laying plans for the return to civilian life of our gallant men and women in the armed services. They must not be demobilized into an environment of inflation and unemployment, to a place on a bread line, or on a corner selling apples. We must, this time, have plans ready—instead of waiting to do a hasty, inefficient, and ill-considered job at the last moment.

I have assured our men in the armed forces that the American people would not let them down when the war is won.

I hope that the Congress will help in carrying out this assurance, for obviously the Executive Branch of the Government cannot do it alone.

May the Congress do its duty in this regard. The American people will insist on fulfilling this American obligation to the men and women in the armed forces who are winning this war for us. Of course, the returning soldier and sailor and marine are a part of the problem of demobilizing the rest of the millions of Americans who have been living in a war economy since 1941. That larger objective of reconverting wartime America to a peacetime basis is one for which your government is laying plans to be submitted to the Congress for action.

But the members of the armed forces have been compelled to make greater economic sacrifice and every other kind of sacrifice than the rest of us, and they are entitled to definite action to help take care of their special problems.

The least to which they are entitled, it seems to me, is something like this: First, mustering-out pay to every member of the armed forces and merchant marine when he or she is honorably discharged, mustering-out pay large enough in each case to cover a reasonable period of time between his discharge and the finding of a new job. Secondly, in case no job is found after diligent search, then unemployment insurance if the individual registers with the United States Employment Service. Third, an opportunity for members of the armed services to get further education or trade training at the cost of the government. Fourth, allowance of credit to all members of the armed forces, under unemployment compensation and Federal old-age and survivors' insurance, for their period of service. For these purposes they ought to be treated as if they had continued their employment in private industry. Fifth, improved and liberalized provisions for hospitalization, for rehabilitation, for medical care of disabled members of the armed forces and the merchant marine. And finally, sufficient pensions for disabled members of the armed forces. Your Government is drawing up other serious, constructive plans for certain immediate forward moves. They concern food, manpower, and other domestic problems that tie in with our armed forces.

Within a few weeks I shall speak with you again in regard to definite actions to be taken by the Executive Branch of the Government, together with specific recommendations for new legislation by the Congress.

All our calculations for the future, however, must be based on clear understanding of the problems involved. And that can be gained only by straight thinking—not guess work, not political manipulation.

I confess that I myself am sometimes bewildered by conflicting statements that I see in the press. One day I read an "authoritative" statement that we will win the war this year, 1943—and the next day comes another statement equally "authoritative," that the war will still be going on in 1949.

Of course, both extremes—of optimism and pessimism—are wrong.

The length of the war will depend upon the uninterrupted continuance of all-out effort on the fighting fronts and here at home, and that effort is all one.

The American soldier doesn't like the necessity of waging war. And yet—if he lays off for a single instant he may lose his own life and sacrifice the lives of his comrades.

By the same token—a worker here at home may not like the driving, wartime conditions under which he has to work and live. And yet—if he gets complacent or indifferent and slacks on his job, he too may sacrifice the lives of American soldiers and contribute to the loss of an important battle.

The next time anyone says to you that this war is "in the bag," or says "it's all over but the shouting," you should ask him these questions: "Are you working full time on your job?" "Are you growing all the food you can?" "Are you buying your limit of war bonds?" "Are you loyally and cheerfully cooperating with your Government in preventing inflation and profiteering, and in making rationing work with fairness to all?"

Because—if your answer is "No"—then the war is going to last a lot longer than you think. The plans we made for the knocking out of Mussolini and his gang have largely succeeded. But we still have to knock out Hitler and his gang, and Tojo and his gang. No one of us pretends that this will be an easy matter.

We still have to defeat Hitler and Tojo on their own home grounds. But this will require a far greater concentration of our national energy and our ingenuity and our skill.

It isn't too much to say that we must pour into this war the entire strength and intelligence and will power of the United States. We are a great nation—a rich nation—but we are not so great or so rich that we can afford to waste our substance or the lives or our men by relaxing along the way.

We shall not settle for less than total victory. That is the determination of every American on the fighting fronts. That must be, and will be, the determination of every American here at home.

Fireside Chat (on the Fifth War Loan Drive)
Washington, D.C., June 12, 1944

When FDR went on the radio on the evening of June 5, 1944 to announce that the Fifth Army had captured Rome, he knew what only a handful of people in the Western Hemisphere knew at that moment, that the first wave of paratroopers had already been dropped behind enemy lines in France, and the huge D-Day invasion force was on its way across the English Channel to the Normandy beaches. With uncertain weather conditions and German defenses of unknown strength, the next several days represented an uneasy period in Washington as the Allies put a million soldiers and the necessary equipment ashore. This was the background for FDR's June 12th speech on behalf of the Fifth World War II Loan Drive then getting under way. For the Commander in Chief, the war not only had to be won, it had to be paid for. Taxes raised less than half of the $321 billion cost of World War II (in 1940s dollars), and their collection in those wartime years did add one new feature to the American fiscal landscape—the withholding of federal income taxes that went into effect in 1943. Money not raised by taxes had to be borrowed, and as war bonds were sold, the national debt rose from $49 billion in 1941 to more than five times that figure by 1945.

Ladies and gentlemen:

All our fighting men overseas today have their appointed stations on the far-flung battlefronts of the world. We at home have ours too. We need, we are proud of, our fighting men—most decidedly. But, during the anxious times ahead, let us not forget that they need us too.

It goes almost without saying that we must continue to forge the weapons of victory—the hundreds of thousands of items, large and small, essential to the waging of the war. This has been the major task from the very start, and it is still a major task. This is the very worst time for any war worker to think of leaving his machine or to look for a peacetime job.

And it goes almost without saying, too, that we must continue to provide our Government with the funds necessary for waging war not only by the payment of taxes—which, after all, is an obligation of American citizenship—but also by the purchase of War Bonds—an act of free choice which every citizen has to make for himself under the guidance of his own conscience.

Whatever else any of us may be doing, the purchase of War Bonds and stamps is something all of us can do and should do to help win the war. I am happy to report tonight that it is something which—something nearly everyone seems to be doing. Although there are now approximately sixty-seven million persons who have or earn some form of income (including the armed forces), eighty-one million persons or their children have already bought war bonds. They have bought more than six hundred million individual bonds. Their purchases have totaled more than thirty-two billion dollars. These are the purchases of individual men, women and children. Anyone who would have said this was possible a few years ago would have been put down as a starry-eyed visionary. But of such visions is the stuff of America fashioned.

Of course, there are always pessimists with us everywhere, a few here and a few there. I am reminded of the fact that after the fall of France in 1940 I asked the Congress for the money for the production by the United States of fifty thousand airplanes per year. Well, I was called crazy—it was said that the figure was fantastic; that it could not be done. And yet today we are building airplanes at the rate of one hundred thousand a year.

There is a direct connection between the Bonds you have bought and the stream of men and equipment now rushing over the English Channel for the liberation of Europe. There is a direct connection between your War Bonds and every part of this global war today.

Tonight, therefore on the opening of this Fifth War Loan Drive, it is appropriate for us to take a broad look at this panorama of world war, for the success or the failure of the drive is going to have so much to do with the speed with which we can accomplish victory and the peace.

While I know that the chief interest tonight is centered on the English Channel and on the beaches and farms and the cities of Normandy, we should not lose sight of the fact that our armed forces are engaged on other battlefronts all over the world, and that no one front can be considered alone without its proper relation to all.

It is worth while, therefore, to make over-all comparisons with the past. Let us compare today with just two years ago—June, 1942. At that time Germany was in control of practically all of Europe, and was steadily driving the Russians back toward the Ural Mountains. Germany was practically in control of North Africa and the Mediterranean, and was beating at the gates of the Suez Canal and the route to India. Italy was still an important military and supply factor — as subsequent, long campaigns have proved.

Japan was in control of the western Aleutian Islands; and in the South Pacific was knocking at the gates of Australia and New Zealand — and also was threatening India. Japan had seized control of nearly one half of the Central Pacific.

American armed forces on land and sea and in the air were still very definitely on the defensive, and in the building-up stage. Our Allies were bearing the heat and the brunt of the attack.

In 1942 Washington heaved a sigh of relief that the first War Bond issue had been cheerfully over-subscribed by the American people. Way back in those days, two years ago, America was still hearing from many "amateur strategists" and political critics, some of whom were doing more good for Hitler than for the United States — two years ago.

But today we are on the offensive all over the world — bringing the attack to our enemies.

In the Pacific, by relentless submarine and naval attacks, and amphibious thrusts, and ever-mounting air attacks, we have deprived the Japs of the power to check the momentum of our ever-growing and ever-advancing military forces. We have reduced the Japs' shipping by more than three million tons. We have overcome their original advantage in the air. We have cut off from a return to the homeland, cut off from that return, tens of thousands of beleaguered Japanese troops who now face starvation or ultimate surrender. And we have cut down their naval strength, so that for many months they have avoided all risk of encounter with our naval forces.

True, we still have a long way to go to Tokyo. But, carrying out our original strategy of eliminating our European enemy first and then turning all our strength to the Pacific, we can force the Japanese to unconditional surrender or to national suicide much more rapidly than has been thought possible.

Turning now to our enemy who is first on the list for destruction — Germany has her back against the wall — in fact three walls at once!

In the south — we have broken the German hold on central Italy. On June fourth, the city of Rome fell to the Allied armies. And allowing the enemy no respite, the Allies are now pressing hard on the heels of the Germans as they retreat northwards in ever-growing confusion.

On the east — our gallant Soviet Allies have driven the enemy back from the lands which were invaded three years ago. The great Soviet armies are now initiating crushing blows.

Overhead—vast Allied air fleets of bombers and fighters have been waging a bitter air war over Germany and Western Europe. They have had two major objectives: to destroy German war industries which maintain the German armies and air forces; and to shoot the German Luftwaffe out of the air. As a result German production has been whittled down continuously, and the German fighter forces now have only a fraction of their former power.

This great air campaign, strategic and tactical, is going to continue— with increasing power.

And on the west—the hammer blow which struck the coast of France last Tuesday morning, less than a week ago, was the culmination of many months of careful planning and strenuous preparation.

Millions of tons of weapons and supplies, hundreds of thousands of men assembled in England, are now being poured into the great battle in Europe.

I think that from the standpoint of our enemy we have achieved the impossible. We have broken through their supposedly impregnable wall in Northern France. But the assault has been costly in men and costly in materials. Some of our landings were desperate adventures; but from advices received so far, the losses were lower than our commanders had estimated would occur. We have established a firm foothold. We are now prepared to meet the inevitable counter-attacks of the Germans—with power and with confidence. And we all pray that we will have far more, soon, than a firm foothold.

Americans have all worked together to make this day possible.

The liberation forces now streaming across the Channel, and up the beaches and through the fields and the forests of France are using thousands and thousands of planes and ships and tanks and heavy guns. They are carrying with them many thousands of items needed for their dangerous, stupendous undertaking. There is a shortage of nothing— nothing! And this must continue.

What has been done in the United States since those days of 1940— when France fell—in raising and equipping and transporting our fighting forces, and in producing weapons and supplies for war, has been nothing short of a miracle. It was largely due to American teamwork— teamwork among capital and labor and agriculture, between the armed forces and the civilian economy—indeed among all of them.

And every one—every man or woman or child—who bought a War Bond helped—and helped mightily!

There are still many people in the United States who have not bought War Bonds, or who have not bought as many as they can afford. Everyone knows for himself whether he falls into that category or not. In some cases his neighbors know too. To the consciences of those people, this appeal by the President of the United States is very much in order.

For all of the things which we use in this war, everything we send to our fighting Allies, costs money—a lot of money. One sure way every man, woman and child can keep faith with those who have given, and are giving, their lives, is to provide the money which is needed to win the final victory.

I urge all Americans to buy War Bonds without stint. Swell the mighty chorus to bring us nearer to victory!

Campaign Speech to the Teamsters Union

Washington, D.C., September 23, 1944

Early in 1944, FDR privately expressed the feeling that he didn't really feel up to a fourth campaign for the presidency, and the hope that by the time the American political season heated up later that year he might not be needed as a candidate. It didn't work out that way. The D-Day landings in June gave promise of final success in Europe, but the end of the war was not yet in sight, and in July, Roosevelt let it be known that he would accept the Democratic party's nomination. Once that hurdle was surmounted, the principal political intrigue of 1944 for the Democrats concerned strengthening the ticket with the replacement of Henry Wallace as vice-president with the capable senator from Missouri, Harry S Truman.

As the campaign against the Republican nominee, Governor Thomas E. Dewey of New York, got under way, FDR faced all of the old political antagonisms, as well as new rumors about his failing health and vigor. Some less than dazzling public appearances hadn't helped. A major political triumph was essential to properly launch the campaign, and in search of just such a springboard, FDR accepted an invitation to give a speech at a Teamsters Union dinner—which was also heard by a huge radio audience—at Washington's Statler Hotel on September 23rd. The speech, like all of his major addresses, went through draft after draft right up until the last possible moment, and the teamsters put FDR in the right fighting mood with a long, thunderous ovation before he went on the air. As pure politics, the speech was a definitive rout, the finest of FDR's career as a campaigner. Doubts about FDR's ability to continue in office were effectively silenced. The Dewey campaign team worked hard, but their biggest liability was possibly the charmless Republican candidate himself. Roosevelt had some respect for Hoover and Landon and even some affection for Wilkie, but only contempt for Dewey. "You ought to hear him," he told speechwriter Robert Sherwood. "He plays the part of the heroic racket-buster in one of those gangster movies. He talks to people as if they were the jury and I were the villain on trial for his life."

   With the Depression a memory, and Eisenhower's army closing in on final victory over Nazi Germany, the prosecutorial approach didn't work for the Republicans in 1944. Six weeks after the speech to the teamsters, FDR had his traditional lucky election night dinner of scrambled eggs, and stayed up at Hyde Park until 4 A.M. tabulating the results from radio news reports as he always did, finally going to bed only annoyed that Dewey hadn't yet publicly conceded. FDR's fourth presidential victory was by a decisive 432 electoral votes to 99, with 53.5% of the popular vote against 46%. Roosevelt was hardly mollified when Dewey finally sent his personal congratulations three days later.

Mr. Tobin—I should say Dan, I always have—ladies and gentlemen. I am very much touched, and I am very happy in your applause, and very happy at the informalities of this dinner with old friends of mine. You know, this is not the first time that we have met together on this basis, and I am particularly happy that this national campaign opens in your presence as it did four years ago. And I don't mind mentioning the fact that Dan Tobin and I are just a little bit superstitious.

   Well, here we are—here we are again—after four years—and what years they have been! You know, I am actually four years older—which is a fact that seems to annoy some people. In fact, in the mathematical field there are millions of Americans who are more than eleven years older than when we started in to clear up the mess that was dumped in our laps in 1933.

   We all know that certain people who make it a practice to depreciate the accomplishments of labor—who even attack labor as unpatriotic—they keep this up usually for three years and six months in a row. But then, for some strange reason—they change their tune—every four years—just before election day. When votes are at stake, they suddenly discover that they really love labor—and that they are anxious to protect labor from its old friends.

   I got quite a laugh, for example—and I am sure that you did—when I read this plank in the Republican platform adopted at their National Convention in Chicago last July:

   "The Republican party accepts the purposes of the National Labor Relations Act, the Wage and Hour Act, the Social Security Act and all other Federal statutes designed to promote and protect the welfare of American working men and women, and we promise a fair and just administration of these laws."

   You know, many of the Republican leaders and Congressmen and candidates, who shouted enthusiastic approval of that plank in that Convention Hall would not even recognize these progressive laws, if they met them in broad daylight. Indeed, they have personally spent years of effort and energy—and much money—in fighting every one of those laws in the Congress, and in the press, and in the courts, ever since this Administration began to advocate them and enact them into legislation. That is a fair example of their insincerity and of their inconsistency.

The whole purpose of Republican oratory these days seems to be to switch labels. The object is to persuade the American people that the Democratic party was responsible for the 1929 crash and the depression, and that the Republican party was responsible for all social progress under the New Deal.

Now, imitation may be the sincerest form of flattery—but I am afraid that in this case it is the most obvious common or garden variety of fraud.

Of course, it is perfectly true that there are enlightened, liberal elements in the Republican party, and they have fought hard and honorably to bring the party up to date and to get it in step with the forward march of American progress. But these liberal elements were not able to drive the Old Guard Republicans from their entrenched positions.

Can the Old Guard pass itself off as the New Deal?

I think not.

We have all seen many marvelous stunts in the circus, but no performing elephant could turn a hand-spring without falling flat on his back.

I need not recount to you the centuries of history which have been crowded into these four years since I saw you last.

There were some—in the Congress and out—who raised their voices against our preparations for defense—before and after 1939—objected to them, raised their voices against them as hysterical war mongering, who cried out against our help to the Allies as provocative and dangerous. We remember the voices. They would like to have us forget them now. But in 1940 and 1941—my, it seems a long time ago—they were loud voices. Happily they were a minority and—fortunately for ourselves, and for the world—they could not stop America.

There are some politicians who kept their heads buried deep in the sand while the storms of Europe and Asia were headed our way, who said that the lend-lease bill "would bring an end"—and I am quoting—"to free government in the United States," and who said, and I am quoting, "only hysteria entertains the idea that Germany, Italy or Japan contemplate war on us." These men—these very men are now asking the

American people to intrust to them the conduct of our foreign policy and our military policy.

What the Republican leaders are now saying in effect is this: "Oh, just forget what we used to say, we have changed our minds now—we have been reading the public opinion polls about these things—and now we know what the American people want." And they say: "Don't leave the task of making the peace to those old men who first urged it and who have already laid the foundations for it, and who have had to fight all of us inch by inch during the last five years to do it. Why, just turn it all over to us. We'll do it so skilfully—that we won't lose a single isolationist vote or a single isolationist campaign contribution."

I think there is one thing that you know, I am too old for that. I cannot talk out of both sides of my mouth at the same time.

The Government of the United States welcomes all sincere supporters of the cause of effective world collaboration in the making of a lasting peace. Millions of Republicans all over the nation are with us—and have been with us—in our unshakeable determination to build the solid structure of peace. And they too will resent this campaign—this campaign talk by those who first woke up to the facts of international life a few short months ago—when they began to study the polls of public opinion.

Those who today have the military responsibility for waging this war in all parts of the globe are not helped by the statements of men who, without responsibility and without the knowledge of the facts, lecture the Chiefs of Staff of the United States as to the best means of dividing our armed forces and our military resources between the Atlantic and Pacific, between the Army and the Navy, and among the Commanding Generals of the different theatres of war. And I may say that those Commanding Generals are making good in a big way.

When I addressed you four years ago, I said this. I said, "I know that America will never be disappointed in its expectation that labor will always continue to do its share of the job—the job we now face, and do it patriotically and effectively and unselfishly."

Today we know that America has not been disappointed. In his Order of the Day when the Allied Armies first landed in Normandy two months ago, General Eisenhower said: "Our home fronts have given us overwhelming superiority in weapons and munitions of war."

The country knows that there is a breed of cats, luckily not too numerous, called labor-baiters. I know that those labor-baiters among the opposition are there, who instead of calling attention to the achievements of labor in this war, prefer to pick on the occasional strikes that have occurred—strikes that have been condemned by every responsible national labor leader. I ought to say, parenthetically, all but one

[John L. Lewis of the United Mine Workers]. And that one labor leader, incidentally, is not conspicuous among my supporters.

Labor-baiters forget that at our peak American labor and management have turned out airplanes at the rate of 109,000 a year; tanks—57,000 a year; combat vessels—573 a year; landing vessels, to get the troops ashore—31,000 a year; cargo ships—19 million tons a year—and Henry Kaiser is here tonight, I am glad to say; and small arms ammunition—oh, I can't understand it, I don't believe you can, either—23 billion rounds a year.

But a strike is news, and generally appears in shrieking headlines—and, of course, they say labor is always to blame. The fact is that since Pearl Harbor only one-tenth of one percent of manhours have been lost by strikes. Can you beat that?

But, you know, even those candidates who burst out in election-year affection for social legislation and for labor in general, still think that you ought to be good boys and stay out of politics. And above all, they hate to see any working man or woman contribute a dollar bill to any wicked political party. Of course, it is all right for large financiers and industrialists and monopolists to contribute tens of thousands of dollars—but their solicitude for that dollar which the men and women in the ranks of labor contribute is always very touching.

They are, of course, perfectly willing to let you vote—unless you happen to be a soldier or a sailor overseas, or a merchant seaman carrying the munitions of war. In that case they have made it pretty hard for you to vote at all—for there are some political candidates who think that they may have a chance of election, if only the total vote is small enough.

And while I am on the subject of voting, let me urge every American citizen—man and woman—to use your sacred privilege of voting, no matter which candidate you expect to support. Our millions of soldiers and sailors and merchant seamen have been handicapped or prevented from voting by those politicians, those candidates who think that they stand to lose by such votes. You here at home have the freedom of the ballot. Irrespective of party, you should register and vote this November. I think that is a matter of plain good citizenship.

Words come easily, but they do not change the record. You are, most of you, old enough to remember what things were like for labor in 1932.

You remember the closed banks and the breadlines and the starvation wages; the foreclosures of homes and farms, and the bankruptcies of business; the "Hoovervilles," and the young men and women of the nation facing a hopeless, jobless future; the closed factories and mines and mills; the ruined and abandoned farms; the stalled railroads, the empty docks; the blank despair of a whole nation—and the utter impotence of the Federal Government.

You remember the long hard road, with its gains and its setbacks, which we have traveled together ever since those days.

Now there are some politicians who do not remember that far back—and there are some who remember but find it convenient to forget. No, the record is not to be washed away that easily.

The opposition in this year has already imported into this campaign a very interesting thing, because it is foreign. They have imported the propaganda technique invented by the dictators abroad. Remember, a number of years ago, there was a book *Mein Kampf* written by Hitler himself. The technique was all set out in Hitler's book—and it was copied by the aggressors of Italy and Japan. According to that technique, you should never use a small falsehood; always a big one for its very fantastic nature would make it more credible—if only you keep repeating it over and over and over again.

Well, let us take some simple illustrations that come to mind. For example, although I rubbed my eyes when I read it, we have been told that it was not a Republican depression, but a Democratic depression from which this nation was saved in 1933—that this Administration—this one—today—is responsible for all the suffering and misery that the history books and the American people have always thought had been brought about during the twelve ill-fated years when the Republican party was in power.

Now, there is an old and somewhat lugubrious adage which says: "Never speak of a rope in the house of a man who has been hanged." In the same way, if I were a Republican leader speaking to a mixed audience, the last word in the whole dictionary that I think I would use is that word "depression."

You know, they pop up all the time. For another example, I learned—much to my amazement—that the policy of this Administration was to keep men in the Army when the war was over, because there might be no jobs for them in civil life.

Well, the very day that this fantastic charge was first made, a formal plan for the method of speedy discharge from the Army had already been announced by the War Department—a plan based on the wishes of the soldiers themselves.

This callous and brazen falsehood about demobilization did, of course, a very simple thing, it was an effort to stimulate fear among American mothers and wives and sweethearts. And, incidentally, it was hardly calculated to bolster the morale of our soldiers and sailors and airmen who are fighting our battles all over the world.

But perhaps the most ridiculous of these campaign falsifications is the one that this Administration failed to prepare for the war that was coming. I doubt whether even Goebbels would have tried that one. For even he would never have dared hope that the voters of America had already forgotten that many of the Republican leaders in the Congress and outside the Congress tried to thwart and block nearly every attempt that this Administration made to warn our people and arm our nation. Some of them called our 50,000 airplane program fantastic. Many of those very same leaders who fought every defense measure that we proposed are still in control of the Republican party—look at their names—were in control of its National Convention in Chicago, and would be in control of the machinery of the Congress and of the Republican party, in the event of a Republican victory this fall.

These Republican leaders have not been content with attacks on me, or my wife, or on my sons. No, not content with that they now include my little dog, Fala. Well, of course, I don't resent attacks, and my family don't resent attacks, but Fala *does* resent them. You know—you know, Fala is Scotch, and being a Scottie, as soon as he learned that the Republican fiction-writers in Congress and out had concocted a story that I had left him behind on the Aleutian Islands and had sent a destroyer back to find him—at a cost to the taxpayers of two or three, or eight or twenty million dollars—his Scotch soul was furious. He has not been the same dog since. I am accustomed to hearing malicious falsehoods about myself—such as that old, worm-eaten chestnut that I have represented myself as indispensable. But I think I have a right to resent, to object to libelous statements about my dog.

Well, I think we all recognize the old technique. The people of this country know the past too well to be deceived into forgetting. Too much is at stake to forget. There are tasks ahead of us which we must now complete with the same will and the same skill and intelligence and devotion that have already led us so far along the road to victory.

There is the task of finishing victoriously this most terrible of all wars as speedily as possible and with the least cost in lives.

There is the task of setting up international machinery to assure that the peace, once established, will not again be broken.

And there is the task that we face here at home—the task of reconverting our economy from the purposes of war to the purposes of peace.

These peace-building tasks were faced once before, nearly a generation ago. They were botched by a Republican administration. That must not happen this time. We will not let it happen this time.

Fortunately, we do not begin from scratch. Much has been done. Much more is under way. The fruits of victory this time will not be apples sold on street corners.

Many months ago this Administration set up necessary machinery for an orderly peace-time demobilization. The Congress has passed much more legislation continuing the agencies needed for demobilization—with additional powers to carry out their functions.

I know that the American people—business and labor and agriculture—have the same will to do for peace what they have done for war. And I know that they can sustain a national income that will assure full production and full employment under our democratic system of private enterprise, with Government encouragement and aid whenever and wherever that is necessary.

The keynote back of all this literature that we read, the keynote of all that we propose to do in reconversion can be found in the one word JOBS.

We shall lease or dispose of our Government-owned plants and facilities and our surplus war property and land, on the basis of how they can best be operated by private enterprise to give jobs to the greatest number.

We shall follow a wage policy that will sustain the purchasing power of labor—for that means more production and more jobs.

You and I know that the present policies on wages and prices were conceived to serve the needs of the great masses of the people. They stopped inflation. They kept prices on a relatively stable level. Through the demobilization period, policies will be carried out with the same objective in mind—to serve the needs of the great masses of the people.

This is not the time in which men can be forgotten as they were in the Republican catastrophe that we inherited. The returning soldiers, the workers by their machines, the farmers in the field, the miners, the men and women in offices and shops, do not intend to be forgotten.

No, they know that they are not surplus. Because they know that they are America.

We must set targets and objectives for the future which will seem impossible—like the airplanes—to those who live in and are weighted down by the dead past.

And for months—and today and in the future we are working and will continue to put forth the logistics of the peace, just as Marshall and King and Arnold, MacArthur, Eisenhower and Nimitz are organizing the logistics of this war.

I think that the victory of the American people and their Allies in this war will be far more than a victory against fascism and reaction and the dead hand of despotism of the past. The victory of the American people and their Allies in this war will be a victory for democracy. It will constitute such an affirmation of the strength and power and vitality of government by the people as history has never before witnessed.

And so, my friends, with that affirmation of the vitality of democratic government behind us, that demonstration of its resilience and its capacity for decision and for action—with that knowledge of our own strength and power—we move forward with God's help to the greatest epoch of free achievement by free men that the world has ever known or imagined possible.

Fourth Inaugural Address
Washington, D.C., January 20, 1945

FDR's Fourth Inaugural differed from the first three in many ways. It was the only one of his held while the country was at war, and it was decided that a simple ceremony, without the typical fanfare, would be more appropriate. This time the oath of office was administered by a new chief justice, Harlan F. Stone; and the ceremony took place on the balcony of the south portico of the White House instead of at the Capitol. The speech was brief and with the hindsight of history sounds somewhat weary, as we know now that when FDR gave it he had less than three months to live.

In early February, 1945, two weeks after his Fourth Inaugural, Roosevelt met with Churchill and Stalin at Yalta in the Crimea to plan the final phase of the war against Germany. The decision to accept only an unconditional surrender was reconfirmed, and the eventual four-power (France, Great Britain, United States, Soviet Union) occupation of Germany was planned. By the time of his return from Yalta, FDR was clearly in failing health. He died of a cerebral hemorrhage at Warm Springs, Georgia on April 12, 1945.

Mr. Chief Justice, Mr. Vice President, my friends, you will understand and, I believe, agree with my wish that the form of this inauguration be simple and its words brief.

We Americans of today, together with our allies, are passing through a period of supreme test. It is a test of our courage—of our resolve—of our wisdom—our essential democracy.

If we meet that test—successfully and honorably—we shall perform a service of historic importance which men and women and children will honor throughout all time.

As I stand here today, having taken the solemn oath of office in the presence of my fellow countrymen—in the presence of our God—I know that it is America's purpose that we shall not fail.

In the days and in the years that are to come we shall work for a just and honorable peace, a durable peace, as today we work and fight for total victory in war.

We can and we will achieve such a peace.

We shall strive for perfection. We shall not achieve it immediately— but we still shall strive. We may make mistakes—but they must never be mistakes which result from faintness of heart or abandonment of moral principle.

I remember that my old schoolmaster, Dr. Peabody, said, in days that seemed to us then to be secure and untroubled: "Things in life will not always run smoothly. Sometimes we will be rising toward the heights— then all will seem to reverse itself and start downward. The great fact to remember is that the trend of civilization itself is forever upward; that a line drawn through the middle of the peaks and the valleys of the centuries always has an upward trend."

Our Constitution of 1787 was not a perfect instrument; it is not perfect yet. But it provided a firm base upon which all manner of men, of all races and colors and creeds, could build our solid structure of democracy.

And so today, in this year of war, 1945, we have learned lessons—at a fearful cost—and we shall profit by them.

We have learned that we cannot live alone, at peace; that our own well-being is dependent on the well-being of other nations far away. We have learned that we must live as men, not as ostriches, nor as dogs in the manger.

We have learned to be citizens of the world, members of the human community.

We have learned the simple truth, as Emerson said, that "The only way to have a friend is to be one."

We can gain no lasting peace if we approach it with suspicion and mistrust or with fear. We can gain it only if we proceed with the understanding, the confidence, and the courage which flow from conviction.

The Almighty God has blessed our land in many ways. He has given our people stout hearts and strong arms with which to strike mighty blows for freedom and truth. He has given to our country a faith which has become the hope of all peoples in an anguished world.

So we pray to Him now for the vision to see our way clearly—to see the way that leads to a better life for ourselves and for all our fellow men—to the achievement of His will to peace on earth.

DOVER·THRIFT·EDITIONS

FICTION

A JOURNAL OF THE PLAGUE YEAR, Daniel Defoe. 192pp. 41919-3
SIX GREAT SHERLOCK HOLMES STORIES, Sir Arthur Conan Doyle. 112pp. 27055-6
SHORT STORIES, Theodore Dreiser. 112pp. 28215-5
SILAS MARNER, George Eliot. 160pp. 29246-0
JOSEPH ANDREWS, Henry Fielding. 288pp. 41588-0
THIS SIDE OF PARADISE, F. Scott Fitzgerald. 208pp. 28999-0
"THE DIAMOND AS BIG AS THE RITZ" AND OTHER STORIES, F. Scott Fitzgerald. 29991-0
MADAME BOVARY, Gustave Flaubert. 256pp. 29257-6
THE REVOLT OF "MOTHER" AND OTHER STORIES, Mary E. Wilkins Freeman. 128pp.
  40428-5
A ROOM WITH A VIEW, E. M. Forster. 176pp. (Available in U.S. only.) 28467-0
WHERE ANGELS FEAR TO TREAD, E. M. Forster. 128pp. (Available in U.S. only.) 27791-7
THE IMMORALIST, André Gide. 112pp. (Available in U.S. only.) 29237-1
HERLAND, Charlotte Perkins Gilman. 128pp. 40429-3
"THE YELLOW WALLPAPER" AND OTHER STORIES, Charlotte Perkins Gilman. 80pp. 29857-4
THE OVERCOAT AND OTHER STORIES, Nikolai Gogol. 112pp. 27057-2
CHELKASH AND OTHER STORIES, Maxim Gorky. 64pp. 40652-0
GREAT GHOST STORIES, John Grafton (ed.). 112pp. 27270-2
DETECTION BY GASLIGHT, Douglas G. Greene (ed.). 272pp. 29928-7
THE MABINOGION, Lady Charlotte E. Guest. 192pp. 29541-9
"THE FIDDLER OF THE REELS" AND OTHER SHORT STORIES, Thomas Hardy. 80pp. 29960-0
THE LUCK OF ROARING CAMP AND OTHER STORIES, Bret Harte. 96pp. 27271-0
THE HOUSE OF THE SEVEN GABLES, Nathaniel Hawthorne. 272pp. 40882-5
THE SCARLET LETTER, Nathaniel Hawthorne. 192pp. 28048-9
YOUNG GOODMAN BROWN AND OTHER STORIES, Nathaniel Hawthorne. 128pp. 27060-2
THE GIFT OF THE MAGI AND OTHER SHORT STORIES, O. Henry. 96pp. 27061-0
THE NUTCRACKER AND THE GOLDEN POT, E. T. A. Hoffmann. 128pp. 27806-9
THE ASPERN PAPERS, Henry James. 112pp. 41922-3
THE BEAST IN THE JUNGLE AND OTHER STORIES, Henry James. 128pp. 27552-3
DAISY MILLER, Henry James. 64pp. 28773-4
THE TURN OF THE SCREW, Henry James. 96pp. 26684-2
WASHINGTON SQUARE, Henry James. 176pp. 40431-5
THE COUNTRY OF THE POINTED FIRS, Sarah Orne Jewett. 96pp. 28196-5
THE AUTOBIOGRAPHY OF AN EX-COLORED MAN, James Weldon Johnson. 112pp. 28512-X
DUBLINERS, James Joyce. 160pp. 26870-5
A PORTRAIT OF THE ARTIST AS A YOUNG MAN, James Joyce. 192pp. 28050-0
THE METAMORPHOSIS AND OTHER STORIES, Franz Kafka. 96pp. 29030-1
THE MAN WHO WOULD BE KING AND OTHER STORIES, Rudyard Kipling. 128pp. 28051-9
YOU KNOW ME AL, Ring Lardner. 128pp. 28513-8
SELECTED SHORT STORIES, D. H. Lawrence. 128pp. 27794-1
GREEN TEA AND OTHER GHOST STORIES, J. Sheridan LeFanu. 96pp. 27795-X
THE CALL OF THE WILD, Jack London. 64pp. 26472-6
FIVE GREAT SHORT STORIES, Jack London. 96pp. 27063-7
THE SEA-WOLF, Jack London. 248pp. 41108-7
WHITE FANG, Jack London. 160pp. 26968-X
DEATH IN VENICE, Thomas Mann. 96pp. (Available in U.S. only.) 28714-9
IN A GERMAN PENSION: 13 Stories, Katherine Mansfield. 112pp. 28719-X
THE NECKLACE AND OTHER SHORT STORIES, Guy de Maupassant. 128pp. 27064-5
BARTLEBY AND BENITO CERENO, Herman Melville. 112pp. 26473-4
THE OIL JAR AND OTHER STORIES, Luigi Pirandello. 96pp. 28459-X
THE GOLD-BUG AND OTHER TALES, Edgar Allan Poe. 128pp. 26875-6
TALES OF TERROR AND DETECTION, Edgar Allan Poe. 96pp. 28744-0

DOVER·THRIFT·EDITIONS

FICTION

THE QUEEN OF SPADES AND OTHER STORIES, Alexander Pushkin. 128pp. 28054-3
THE STORY OF AN AFRICAN FARM, Olive Schreiner. 256pp. 40165-0
FRANKENSTEIN, Mary Shelley. 176pp. 28211-2
THE JUNGLE, Upton Sinclair. 320pp. (Available in U.S. only.) 41923-1
THREE LIVES, Gertrude Stein. 176pp. (Available in U.S. only.) 28059-4
THE BODY SNATCHER AND OTHER TALES, Robert Louis Stevenson. 80pp. 41924-X
THE STRANGE CASE OF DR. JEKYLL AND MR. HYDE, Robert Louis Stevenson. 64pp.
   26688-5
TREASURE ISLAND, Robert Louis Stevenson. 160pp. 27559-0
GULLIVER'S TRAVELS, Jonathan Swift. 240pp. 29273-8
THE KREUTZER SONATA AND OTHER SHORT STORIES, Leo Tolstoy. 144pp. 27805-0
THE WARDEN, Anthony Trollope. 176pp. 40076-X
FIRST LOVE AND DIARY OF A SUPERFLUOUS MAN, Ivan Turgenev. 96pp. 28775-0
FATHERS AND SONS, Ivan Turgenev. 176pp. 40073-5
ADVENTURES OF HUCKLEBERRY FINN, Mark Twain. 224pp. 28061-6
THE ADVENTURES OF TOM SAWYER, Mark Twain. 192pp. 40077-8
THE MYSTERIOUS STRANGER AND OTHER STORIES, Mark Twain. 128pp. 27069-6
HUMOROUS STORIES AND SKETCHES, Mark Twain. 80pp. 29279-7
AROUND THE WORLD IN EIGHTY DAYS, Jules Verne. 160pp. 41111-7
CANDIDE, Voltaire (François-Marie Arouet). 112pp. 26689-3
GREAT SHORT STORIES BY AMERICAN WOMEN, Candace Ward (ed.). 192pp. 28776-9
"THE COUNTRY OF THE BLIND" AND OTHER SCIENCE-FICTION STORIES, H. G. Wells. 160pp.
   (Not available in Europe or United Kingdom.) 29569-9
THE ISLAND OF DR. MOREAU, H. G. Wells. 112pp. (Not available in Europe or United
   Kingdom.) 29027-1
THE INVISIBLE MAN, H. G. Wells. 112pp. (Not available in Europe or United Kingdom.)
   27071-8
THE TIME MACHINE, H. G. Wells. 80pp. (Not available in Europe or United Kingdom.)
   28472-7
THE WAR OF THE WORLDS, H. G. Wells. 160pp. (Not available in Europe or United
   Kingdom.) 29506-0
ETHAN FROME, Edith Wharton. 96pp. 26690-7
SHORT STORIES, Edith Wharton. 128pp. 28235-X
THE AGE OF INNOCENCE, Edith Wharton. 288pp. 29803-5
THE PICTURE OF DORIAN GRAY, Oscar Wilde. 192pp. 27807-7
JACOB'S ROOM, Virginia Woolf. 144pp. (Not available in Europe or United Kingdom.)
   40109-X
MONDAY OR TUESDAY: Eight Stories, Virginia Woolf. 64pp. (Not available in Europe or
   United Kingdom.) 29453-6

NONFICTION

POETICS, Aristotle. 64pp. 29577-X
POLITICS, Aristotle. 368pp. 41424-8
NICOMACHEAN ETHICS, Aristotle. 256pp. 40096-4
MEDITATIONS, Marcus Aurelius. 128pp. 29823-X
THE LAND OF LITTLE RAIN, Mary Austin. 96pp. 29037-9
THE DEVIL'S DICTIONARY, Ambrose Bierce. 144pp. 27542-6
THE ANALECTS, Confucius. 128pp. 28484-0
CONFESSIONS OF AN ENGLISH OPIUM EATER, Thomas De Quincey. 80pp. 28742-4
THE SOULS OF BLACK FOLK, W. E. B. Du Bois. 176pp. 28041-1

DOVER·THRIFT·EDITIONS

NONFICTION

NARRATIVE OF THE LIFE OF FREDERICK DOUGLASS, Frederick Douglass. 96pp. 28499-9
SELF-RELIANCE AND OTHER ESSAYS, Ralph Waldo Emerson. 128pp. 27790-9
THE LIFE OF OLAUDAH EQUIANO, OR GUSTAVUS VASSA, THE AFRICAN, Olaudah Equiano. 192pp. 40661-X
THE AUTOBIOGRAPHY OF BENJAMIN FRANKLIN, Benjamin Franklin. 144pp. 29073-5
TOTEM AND TABOO, Sigmund Freud. 176pp. (Not available in Europe or United Kingdom.) 40434-X
LOVE: A Book of Quotations, Herb Galewitz (ed.). 64pp. 40004-2
PRAGMATISM, William James. 128pp. 28270-8
THE STORY OF MY LIFE, Helen Keller. 80pp. 29249-5
TAO TE CHING, Lao Tze. 112pp. 29792-6
GREAT SPEECHES, Abraham Lincoln. 112pp. 26872-1
THE PRINCE, Niccolò Machiavelli. 80pp. 27274-5
THE SUBJECTION OF WOMEN, John Stuart Mill. 112pp. 29601-6
SELECTED ESSAYS, Michel de Montaigne. 96pp. 29109-X
UTOPIA, Sir Thomas More. 96pp. 29583-4
BEYOND GOOD AND EVIL: Prelude to a Philosophy of the Future, Friedrich Nietzsche. 176pp. 29868-X
THE BIRTH OF TRAGEDY, Friedrich Nietzsche. 96pp. 28515-4
COMMON SENSE, Thomas Paine. 64pp. 29602-4
SYMPOSIUM AND PHAEDRUS, Plato. 96pp. 27798-4
THE TRIAL AND DEATH OF SOCRATES: Four Dialogues, Plato. 128pp. 27066-1
A MODEST PROPOSAL AND OTHER SATIRICAL WORKS, Jonathan Swift. 64pp. 28759-9
CIVIL DISOBEDIENCE AND OTHER ESSAYS, Henry David Thoreau. 96pp. 27563-9
SELECTIONS FROM THE JOURNALS (Edited by Walter Harding), Henry David Thoreau. 96pp. 28760-2
WALDEN; OR, LIFE IN THE WOODS, Henry David Thoreau. 224pp. 28495-6
NARRATIVE OF SOJOURNER TRUTH, Sojourner Truth. 80pp. 29899-X
THE THEORY OF THE LEISURE CLASS, Thorstein Veblen. 256pp. 28062-4
DE PROFUNDIS, Oscar Wilde. 64pp. 29308-4
OSCAR WILDE'S WIT AND WISDOM: A Book of Quotations, Oscar Wilde. 64pp. 40146-4
UP FROM SLAVERY, Booker T. Washington. 160pp. 28738-6
A VINDICATION OF THE RIGHTS OF WOMAN, Mary Wollstonecraft. 224pp. 29036-0

PLAYS

PROMETHEUS BOUND, Aeschylus. 64pp. 28762-9
THE ORESTEIA TRILOGY: Agamemnon, The Libation-Bearers and The Furies, Aeschylus. 160pp. 29242-8
LYSISTRATA, Aristophanes. 64pp. 28225-2
WHAT EVERY WOMAN KNOWS, James Barrie. 80pp. (Not available in Europe or United Kingdom.) 29578-8
THE CHERRY ORCHARD, Anton Chekhov. 64pp. 26682-6
THE SEA GULL, Anton Chekhov. 64pp. 40656-3
THE THREE SISTERS, Anton Chekhov. 64pp. 27544-2
UNCLE VANYA, Anton Chekhov. 64pp. 40159-6
THE WAY OF THE WORLD, William Congreve. 80pp. 27787-9
BACCHAE, Euripides. 64pp. 29580-X
MEDEA, Euripides. 64pp. 27548-5

DOVER·THRIFT·EDITIONS

PLAYS

THE MIKADO, William Schwenck Gilbert. 64pp. 27268-0
FAUST, PART ONE, Johann Wolfgang von Goethe. 192pp. 28046-2
THE INSPECTOR GENERAL, Nikolai Gogol. 80pp. 28500-6
SHE STOOPS TO CONQUER, Oliver Goldsmith. 80pp. 26867-5
A DOLL'S HOUSE, Henrik Ibsen. 80pp. 27062-9
GHOSTS, Henrik Ibsen. 64pp. 29852-3
HEDDA GABLER, Henrik Ibsen. 80pp. 26469-6
THE WILD DUCK, Henrik Ibsen. 96pp. 41116-8
VOLPONE, Ben Jonson. 112pp. 28049-7
DR. FAUSTUS, Christopher Marlowe. 64pp. 28208-2
THE MISANTHROPE, Molière. 64pp. 27065-3
ANNA CHRISTIE, Eugene O'Neill. 80pp. 29985-6
BEYOND THE HORIZON, Eugene O'Neill. 96pp. 29085-9
THE EMPEROR JONES, Eugene O'Neill. 64pp. 29268-1
THE LONG VOYAGE HOME AND OTHER PLAYS, Eugene O'Neill. 80pp. 28755-6
RIGHT YOU ARE, IF YOU THINK YOU ARE, Luigi Pirandello. 64pp. (Not available in Europe or United Kingdom.) 29576-1
SIX CHARACTERS IN SEARCH OF AN AUTHOR, Luigi Pirandello. 64pp. (Not available in Europe or United Kingdom.) 29992-9
PHÈDRE, Jean Racine. 64pp. 41927-4
HANDS AROUND, Arthur Schnitzler. 64pp. 28724-6
ANTONY AND CLEOPATRA, William Shakespeare. 128pp. 40062-X
AS YOU LIKE IT, William Shakespeare. 80pp. 40432-3
HAMLET, William Shakespeare. 128pp. 27278-8
HENRY IV, William Shakespeare. 96pp. 29584-2
JULIUS CAESAR, William Shakespeare. 80pp. 26876-4
KING LEAR, William Shakespeare. 112pp. 28058-6
LOVE'S LABOUR'S LOST, William Shakespeare. 64pp. 41929-0
MACBETH, William Shakespeare. 96pp. 27802-6
MEASURE FOR MEASURE, William Shakespeare. 96pp. 40889-2
THE MERCHANT OF VENICE, William Shakespeare. 96pp. 28492-1
A MIDSUMMER NIGHT'S DREAM, William Shakespeare. 80pp. 27067-X
MUCH ADO ABOUT NOTHING, William Shakespeare. 80pp. 28272-4
OTHELLO, William Shakespeare. 112pp. 29097-2
RICHARD III, William Shakespeare. 112pp. 28747-5
ROMEO AND JULIET, William Shakespeare. 96pp. 27557-4
THE TAMING OF THE SHREW, William Shakespeare. 96pp. 29765-9
THE TEMPEST, William Shakespeare. 96pp. 40658-X
TWELFTH NIGHT; OR, WHAT YOU WILL, William Shakespeare. 80pp. 29290-8
ARMS AND THE MAN, George Bernard Shaw. 80pp. (Not available in Europe or United Kingdom.) 26476-9
HEARTBREAK HOUSE, George Bernard Shaw. 128pp. (Not available in Europe or United Kingdom.) 29291-6
PYGMALION, George Bernard Shaw. 96pp. (Available in U.S. only.) 28222-8
THE RIVALS, Richard Brinsley Sheridan. 96pp. 40433-1
THE SCHOOL FOR SCANDAL, Richard Brinsley Sheridan. 96pp. 26687-7
ANTIGONE, Sophocles. 64pp. 27804-2
OEDIPUS AT COLONUS, Sophocles. 64pp. 40659-8
OEDIPUS REX, Sophocles. 64pp. 26877-2

DOVER·THRIFT·EDITIONS

PLAYS

ELECTRA, Sophocles. 64pp. 28482-4

MISS JULIE, August Strindberg. 64pp. 27281-8

THE PLAYBOY OF THE WESTERN WORLD AND RIDERS TO THE SEA, J. M. Synge. 80pp. 27562-0

THE DUCHESS OF MALFI, John Webster. 96pp. 40660-1

THE IMPORTANCE OF BEING EARNEST, Oscar Wilde. 64pp. 26478-5

LADY WINDERMERE'S FAN, Oscar Wilde. 64pp. 40078-6

BOXED SETS

FAVORITE JANE AUSTEN NOVELS: *Pride and Prejudice, Sense and Sensibility* and *Persuasion* (Complete and Unabridged), Jane Austen. 800pp. 29748-9

BEST WORKS OF MARK TWAIN: Four Books, Dover. 624pp. 40226-6

EIGHT GREAT GREEK TRAGEDIES: Six Books, Dover. 480pp. 40203-7

FIVE GREAT ENGLISH ROMANTIC POETS, Dover. 496pp. 27893-X

FIVE GREAT PLAYS, Dover. 368pp. 27179-X

47 GREAT SHORT STORIES: Stories by Poe, Chekhov, Maupassant, Gogol, O. Henry, and Twain, Dover. 688pp. 27178-1

GREAT AFRICAN-AMERICAN WRITERS: Seven Books, Dover. 704pp. 29995-3

GREAT AMERICAN NOVELS, Dover. 720pp. 28665-7

GREAT ENGLISH NOVELS, Dover. 704pp. 28666-5

GREAT IRISH WRITERS: Five Books, Dover. 672pp. 29996-1

GREAT MODERN WRITERS: Five Books, Dover. 720pp. (Available in U.S. only.) 29458-7

GREAT WOMEN POETS: 4 Complete Books, Dover. 256pp. (Available in U.S. only.) 28388-7

MASTERPIECES OF RUSSIAN LITERATURE: Seven Books, Dover. 880pp. 40665-2

SEVEN GREAT ENGLISH VICTORIAN POETS: Seven Volumes, Dover. 592pp. 40204-5

SIX GREAT AMERICAN POETS: Poems by Poe, Dickinson, Whitman, Longfellow, Frost, and Millay, Dover. 512pp. (Available in U.S. only.) 27425-X

38 SHORT STORIES BY AMERICAN WOMEN WRITERS: Five Books, Dover. 512pp. 29459-5

26 GREAT TALES OF TERROR AND THE SUPERNATURAL, Dover. 608pp. (Available in U.S. only.) 27891-3

All books complete and unabridged. All 5³⁄₁₆" x 8¹⁄₄," paperbound. Available at your book dealer, online at **www.doverpublications.com**, or by writing to Dept. GI, Dover Publications, Inc., 31 East 2nd Street, Mineola, NY 11501. For current price information or for free catalogs (please indicate field of interest), write to Dover Publications or log on to **www.doverpublications.com** and see every Dover book in print. Dover publishes more than 500 books each year on science, elementary and advanced mathematics, biology, music, art, literary history, social sciences, and other areas.